Music Outside the Lines

Music Outside the Lines

*Ideas for Composing
in K-12 Music Classrooms*

Maud Hickey

OXFORD
UNIVERSITY PRESS

OXFORD
UNIVERSITY PRESS

Oxford University Press is a department of the University of Oxford. It furthers the University's objective
of excellence in research, scholarship, and education by publishing worldwide.

Oxford   New York
Auckland   Cape Town   Dar es Salaam   Hong Kong   Karachi
Kuala Lumpur   Madrid   Melbourne   Mexico City   Nairobi
New Delhi   Shanghai   Taipei   Toronto

With offices in
Argentina   Austria   Brazil   Chile   Czech Republic   France   Greece
Guatemala   Hungary   Italy   Japan   Poland   Portugal   Singapore
South Korea   Switzerland   Thailand   Turkey   Ukraine   Vietnam

Oxford is a registered trade mark of Oxford University Press in the UK and certain other countries.

Published in the United States of America by
Oxford University Press
198 Madison Avenue, New York, NY 10016

Library of Congress Cataloging-in-Publication Data
Hickey, Maud.
Music outside the lines : ideas for composing in K-12 music classrooms / Maud Hickey.
p.   cm.
Includes bibliographical references and index.
ISBN 978-0-19-982677-3 (hardcover : alk. paper) — ISBN 978-0-19-982679-7 (pbk. : alk. paper)
1. School music—Instruction and study. 2. Composition (Music) I. Title.
MT155.H55 2012
781.3071dc23   2011052882

Preface

This book has been in the works for a very long time. The genesis for it likely goes back to when I was teaching band in a small town in Wisconsin. It was in this circumstance that I first began to wonder about the lack of creative thinking that was taking place in my band room. *What's wrong with this classroom if I am the only person here making the musical decisions (creative or otherwise)?* My pursuit for the answer to the question led me down the path to where I sit today: teaching teachers in higher education about ways in which we can infuse more creative thinking—through improvisation and composition—into our music classrooms. On this journey I have experimented by teaching composition and improvisation to many, many different students, of all ages and backgrounds, and in all kinds of classrooms and spaces. My recent work has brought me into urban facilities and detention centers for high-needs young men and women where I see the positive power of imaginative musical thinking magnified.

When I present my ideas to in-service or preservice teachers now, I feel like what I do is just so perfectly normal. Yet I'm often surprised when I learn that these ideas are still new and that there is still a long way to go to make music composition and improvisation an integral part of music education.

All of my teaching experiences have only strengthened my conviction that creative music making simply must be at the very center of every child's music education. I have observed repeatedly the joy, delight, passion, enthusiasm, patience, concentration and dedication that the children and adults I have worked with exhibit when given the opportunity to improvise and compose. So I want to thank them for giving me the opportunity to try out all of my crazy ideas, as this project would not be remotely possible without their willingness to play along. Unfortunately, none of them will get any credit for writing this book, but they ultimately shaped my thoughts, strengthened my belief in the power of music composition, and taught me what works so that I now can share with others.

A project like this could not come to fruition after all of these years without many people who have been instrumental in supporting and helping me (directly or indirectly). I have had the good fortune of working with wonderful colleagues and students over the years that have listened patiently as I tried to convince them of my ideas. They have also thoughtfully argued with me and challenged me to think even more critically and carefully about my convictions and notions about teaching composition and improvisation. And they have encouraged me to persevere when I wanted to just give up.

I would be remiss without mentioning and thanking my colleague Dr. Janet Barrett, who is responsible for sparking many of the interdisciplinary composing activities that are presented in this book. Her book, *Sound Ways of Knowing: Music in the Interdisciplinary Curriculum* (Barrett, McCoy & Veblan, 1997) also provided a model for this book because of its eloquent approach to combining both theory and practice. She also sets a standard of thinking and writing that I will forever try to reach.

Thanks to Norm Hirschy for his timely and encouraging feedback from the beginning to the end of this project and to Erica Woods Tucker for her amazing editing eye (both at Oxford University Press). I also thank independent artist Wendy Griffiths for the design of my some of the figures in the book.

What better inspiration for cover art on a book about children's music inventions than from children themselves? Thank you to my sweet grandchildren, Noah and Maya, for not only providing the cover art, but also making up songs for me whenever I asked!

Finally I would like to dedicate this book to the wonderful friends and family that I am so blessed to have. And more specifically . . .

To the memory of my dad, who taught me to work really hard but always with a sense of humor;

To my mom, whose model of strength and wisdom continues to be a lifelong goal;

And, finally, to Fred, my husband (as well as editor, golf partner, chef, and friend). He is brilliant, patient, encouraging, kind, funny, and loving: the best kind of life partner one could ever ask for.

I have little interest in teaching you what I know.
I wish to stimulate you to tell me what *you* know.
In my office toward you I am simply trying
to improve my own environment.

Robert Henri, *The Art Spirit*

Contents

Music Outside the Lines

1

Introduction

> The teacher must convince his students that the study of composition will not make them experts or acknowledged judges, that its only purpose is to help them understand music better, to obtain that pleasure which is inherent in the art.
>
> ARNOLD SCHOENBERG, *Style & Idea:*
> *Selected writings of Arnold Schoenberg*

Why Bother?

I have yet to meet a child who could not or would not compose when asked, just as I've never met a child who could not or would not get joy from listening to music, or singing, or performing music on an instrument. Making up music is as natural to children as making up stories and games, or creating original artwork with finger paints and crayons. Yet music composition has not been included as a regular part of the school music curriculum in the United States. In fact, the idea of a person who is both performer and composer at the same time has nearly vanished from Western music since its normalcy only 200 years ago.[1]

Although we can rightfully boast about North America's vast success in producing phenomenal school bands, orchestras and choirs, and professional-level performance musicians who have come through the ranks of these school program ever since the inception of school music education in the early 1800s, we are probably the least successful when it comes to teaching the art of music creation through improvisation and composition. Because of the lack of exposure to music composition in K–12 music classrooms, the natural proclivity and excitement toward music composition fades as students go through formal and school music education. It is a self-perpetuating cycle that we are caught in, as the music teachers themselves have never composed through their education and therefore avoid it in the classroom (and likely send a message that it is something very specialized). If we want to change this condition, then there is an urgent need to begin music composition activities early, often, and in a systematic fashion in our school music curricula as well as in higher education. Music composition (as well as improvisation) needs to be embedded into the experience of every music education undergraduate, and I would argue, those majoring in performance as well.

The absence of composition in music education settings seems curious, especially if we compare our approach of teaching music to that of teaching our sister creative art: visual art. The following scenario illustrates the striking difference between music and visual art education when we imagine teaching visual art in public school in the same way we teach our young musicians.

Beginning Art Class Scenario

On the first day of "painting" class, students walk excitedly into the art classroom carrying their expensive, new (rented of course) paintbrushes in carefully identified cases. Ms. Easington, the teacher, warns the children not to open their cases: "Please set your cases on the table with the handle on the down side, and *do not* open the case until I tell you to." It takes several minutes to teach the children to open their cases properly and to take out the paintbrushes and hold them in the correct manner. They repeat taking out the brush and putting it back several times until Ms. Easington is absolutely sure the children understand. At the end of this first lesson, Ms. Easington gives instruction for the children to practice this "exercise" every day until the next lesson. Subsequent lessons of course get the children painting, but in a very careful and prescribed manner. The paintbrush *must* be held correctly, and the students must paint by number and work to stay *in the lines* of the very basic circles, squares, and triangles! By the end of the first semester, most of the children have memorized four basic colors with their corresponding numbers (blue = 1, red = 2, yellow = 3, green = 4; this is as abstract and random as the standard notation for a quarter note) and are getting quite good at staying in the lines.

At the end of the fifth grade, many of the children have memorized eight colors (and their corresponding numbers), and some children are getting quite good at painting by number and staying in lines, which are increasingly more complex than the beginning basic shapes. Exhibited in the school hallways are basic (somewhat simple and boring) geometric patterns, all exactly alike with the corresponding colors carefully within the lines of squares, circles, and triangles.

Of course a few children do not have the fine motor skills, memorization skills, and/or patience to follow this routine and give up on practicing and decide to drop visual art for the rest of their school career. (Some of these students, however, eventually get together to form a successful company that designs computer graphics for other web-based companies; with no place to work in their school, these highly motivated and successful students work out of a garage on their parents' old Apple computers.)

This natural attrition most often peaks between the middle school and high school years, because the specialty for painting at the high school becomes very complex and more time consuming. The painting students are asked to paint not only complicated "paint-by-number" templates of the great masters (such as Van Gogh's *flowers* and Monet's *fruit*) but also are required to help the athletic department by painting the mascot on the gymnasium wall and school bleachers. The commitment is great, and only a minority of high school students with the determination and special talent stay with this visual art program.

As absurd as this visual art education scenario may seem, it is somewhat characteristic of the approach we take in instrumental music education in the United States. It is also reminiscent of general music classes in which teachers might allow students to read only previously written music ("paint by number"). This scenario is the impetus for the title of this book—that is, music classes are replete with playing "inside the lines" but lack any room for creative playing and making music "outside of the lines."

Hopefully, this may be changing with a relatively recent interest in and focus on music composition as part of a child's total music education. Though the initial thrust toward more creative music education of the 1960s (Benson, 1967; Burton, 1990; Contemporary Music Project, 1965, 1966; Mark, 1996; Thomas, 1970) seemed to have ended abruptly in the 1970s, it never lost its impact. Creative teachers continued to experiment with more innovative approaches to curricula by including composition and improvisation in their classrooms, and the advent of computer music technology in the 1990s supported these efforts even further. Teachers are much more aware of the need for music composition, partly because of the comprehensive National Standards for Music Education (Music Educators National Conference [MENC], 1994) and now more regularly include composing activities in their daily plans. And it is not at all unusual to hear student compositions being played at local, district and state festivals and conferences. What is needed now, more than ever, are resources for teachers to continue enriching their students' musical lives with music composition.

The Need for Materials

The National Standards for Music Education (MENC, 1994) include composition and improvisation as two of the nine standards. MENC has worked at providing additional documents to support the implementation of the standards. For example, the *Performance Standards for Music* (MENC, 1996) provides sample benchmark assessment strategies and corresponding sample achievement levels for each of the content standards. The book *Benchmark Student Performances in Music: Composing and Arranging* (MENC, 2001) is the first publication in a new series that offers sample assessment strategies together with descriptions of student responses at the basic, proficient, and advanced levels for music composition and improvisation at grades 4, 8, and 12. The publication features examples of student work corresponding with the strategies to assist music educators in making judgments about students' progress toward national, state, or local standards. Although these materials support composition in schools, many more are needed to give teachers confidence to make music composition a regular part of their daily music curriculum.

In 2000 Bennett Reimer organized a "Northwestern University Music Education Leadership Seminar" around the topic of music composition in the schools at Northwestern University in Evanston, Illinois. This seminar brought together scholars in music education who have focused on research and practice of music composition in education. The result of the 5-day think tank was a book published by MENC (Hickey, 2003) that provides recent thoughts from leaders in music education who value the importance of music composition with children.

There is still, however, a need for quality materials to aid teachers in teaching music composition in their studios and classrooms, especially in the United States. Historically, texts by Murray Schafer (e.g., 1986, 1992) and John Paynter (Paynter, 1992; Paynter & Aston, 1970)—as well as many of the activities I include in this text and continue to use with children—have positively influenced many teachers in providing creative music activities in classrooms. However, as of this writing I am aware of only a few fairly recent books for aiding teachers in this endeavor: *Composing in the Classroom*, by David Bramhall (1989), *Learning to Compose*, by John Howard (1990), *Composing Matters*, by Patrick Allen (2002), and *Sounds in Space, Sounds in Time: Projects in Listening, Improvising and Composing*, by Richard Vella (2003). Unfortunately, the first two books are out of print, and the second two are published in England, making them expensive and somewhat difficult to obtain. Because the music education system in the United Kingdom includes music composition as an integral part of their music curricula, and has a long history of doing such, it is not surprising that most materials for teachers are published there.

In the United States, other than texts written for academic (university) composers or the popular press (e.g., *Music Composition for Dummies* [Jarrett & Day, 2008] and *Songwriting for Dummies* [Peterik, Austin, & Bickford, 2002]), there is only one recent text published by authors in the United States intended for public school music teachers: *Minds on Music: Composition for Creative and Critical Thinking*, by Michelle Kaschub and Janice Smith (2009). Another book, *Outside the Line: A New Approach to Composing in the Classroom* (Burrows, 2007), for grades 2–6, is out of print. Kaschub and Smith's book, as well as those mentioned above, are hopefully the start of many more materials to come that will help teachers feel more comfortable making music composition an integral part of the K–12 music education landscape.

In order to move music education forward to a place where music composition becomes a regular part of music classrooms in the United States, teachers need to understand why composition is so fundamental to music learning and what students are capable of as composers; and they need materials with ideas for including music composition as a regular part of their curriculum. The intent of this book is to provide this information and more. In the remainder of this chapter, I offer ideas on what music and music composition means in the context of teaching music, provide information on creative thinking, discuss differences between music composition for children and professional composers, and conclude with the notion that music composition is essential for our students' creative musical growth.

Composition Is . . .

When teaching music composition, one of the first things that I ask my students to do is to define *music* and to define *music composition*.[2] This exercise invariably underscores the array of possible definitions for each and provides grist for meaningful and educational debates. The teachers and preservice teachers I work with have all been trained in the classical "conservatory" tradition, so they often place music composition erroneously into a narrow field of study in which the only people who are really capable are those who have had years of specialized education. This separation of music composition from music making into its own *category*, as a specialty that can only be honed through years of focused education and practice, places music composition outside of the realm of classroom or studio music in the minds of many teachers. Students invariably learn through this ill-conceived notion that music composition requires special status and training. Ask a typical 5-year-old child to compose, and there will be no hesitation, but this uninhibited behavior disappears almost completely by the time he or she reaches secondary school, perhaps because the child has not been given the opportunity to compose in the music classroom.

Early in the process of teaching music, it is important to break down flawed yet steadfast assumptions of what music is and what it means to compose music. I enjoy observing the rich learning that occurs as my university students debate among themselves and struggle to come up with acceptable definitions of *music* and *music composition*.[3] The definitions that eventually emerge are often similar to the definitions that I ultimately share with students. Perhaps the most succinct (and sufficiently vague) definition comes from John Cage: "The material of music is sound and silence. Integrating these is composing" (1961, p. 62).

This simple definition makes it clear that any person is capable of composing music,[4] and that playing around with sound is central to this process. Music composition is simply organizing music parts into logical, interesting, and feelingful form. To think creatively and organize sounds into something that is interesting is what makes music composition challenging, fun, and educational for children and adults alike. It involves thoughtful musical behaviors such as careful listening, exploration, divergent thinking, critical decision making, and aesthetic craftsmanship. It is with this philosophy and very basic definition that I approach music composition with students and have found it to be extremely useful to begin this way. But to do so well, it helps to understand a bit about the creative process in music and in general.

Creative Thinking in Music

Creative thinking in music is different from what one might traditionally think of as musical aptitude or "talent." Although one might have tremendous talent to perform flawlessly a range of technically difficult etudes on an instrument, creative thinking in music involves producing new ideas. Musical talent may certainly aid in the production of original and interesting musical products, but a "musically talented" individual may not be very creative. And having students compose or improvise (create new musical ideas) does not necessarily mean that teachers are stimulating creative musical thinking. It is not difficult to imagine a painfully *non*creative music composition lesson. Conversely, being musically creative does not necessarily manifest itself only through music composition or improvisation activities; one could be a musically creative performer or listener as well.

If teachers want to use music composition as an outlet for creative musical thinking, then how can they best encourage their students to think creatively through music composition? What makes a musical student more or less creative? An understanding of concepts from both the field of music as well as creativity will aid in answering these important questions to help teachers feel confident that they are nurturing creative thinking in students through the activity of music composition.

Let's begin by defining *creativity* and *creative thinking*. A simple (hence favorite) definition for creativity is this: "Creativity is a basic human instinct to make that which is new" (Piirto, 1998, p. 41). All humans are born with this potential to create something new or original. For those brought up in an optimal environment (a supportive home, school, and cultural environment), this natural inclination might manifest itself in a domain for which a person has talent as well as exposure, such as in music, or visual art, or science.

Creative musical thinking involves the ability to think imaginatively (creatively) in sound and to manipulate and create *new* and interesting musical ideas. As musicians call upon their creative intelligence in music, they are thinking mostly divergently, rather than convergently, about putting together new sound possibilities. Convergent thinking is the ability to think logically to find the one best solution to a problem, whereas divergent thinking does not require one correct answer, but the ability to render many possible answers. Music composition and improvisation require both kinds of thinking, but offer the best opportunities for students to exercise their divergent, or creative, musical thinking.

Creativity is a valued trait, and often assumed to be synonymous with the arts. However, the adjective *creative* alone can be confusing because of the vast possibilities of meanings. This term might be used to describe a musical product (creative composition or improvisation), personality traits (creative people), or thinking styles (creative processes). *Creative* can also be used to describe a "place," such as a classroom or studio where teaching takes place. The creative product, person, process, and place will be described in the paragraphs that follow.

Creative Product

The creative product is the tangible result of the creative thinking process. In the domain of music, the creative product might be an original composition, improvisation, or even originally nuanced performance of a standard concerto. In most of the myriad definitions of creative products, two adjectives—*original* and *useful*—are used consistently. A creative product is one that is both novel to its creator *and* appropriate or aesthetically interesting in the context of its domain (Mayer, 1999). A product that is only original (imagine that I go to the piano and plunk out a series of random notes that have never been plunked out before), but is in no way or intention interesting, is simply original. *Creative* implies not only *novel*, but also *appropriate* or aesthetically interesting within the domain.

Of course that which is aesthetically interesting in a domain such as music may not be recognized as such until many years later. Indeed, creative products are socially and historically contextual, and their value may change within and between social and historical contexts. In the milieu of a third-grade classroom, the most creative musical compositions will be original and interesting relative to the world of 9-year-old children. As teachers, we want to encourage students to be thoughtful and creative about their music compositions, to think about the intent of the product, and to be able to reflect upon this intent. Teachers should not discourage "strange-sounding" musical compositions in the classroom, but encourage students to reflect upon their creative products in ways that make them think about their audiences and the effects of their products on their audiences. The issue of assessment of the creative product in music (musical composition) will be covered in the next chapter.

Creative Person

Much of what we know about creative people has been compiled from the study of the most creative people in our society both past and present (e.g., Gardner, 1993; Simonton, 1987, 1991, 1999). Analyses of these findings provide us with some common characteristics of creative people, including the following: risk taking; humorous; independent; curious; attraction to ambiguity, complexity, and novelty; open-mindedness; capacity for fantasy; and heightened perception (Davis, 2004; Feist, 1999). There are also potentially negative traits associated with the creative personality as well. These include the following: aloofness, distractible, compulsive, sloppy, and rebellious (Davis, 2004).

Oftentimes little patience is shown for the creative personality and little time is given for creative processes in daily classroom routines. Supporting creative personality characteristics such as those described above is not easy because it is clear that some of these traits are not conducive to maintaining quiet and orderly classrooms. The personality characteristics of the class troublemaker might also characterize that student as the most creative. An awareness of the creative potentials of disruptive students may perhaps help teachers deal better with their behavior. This is not to say that all troublemakers are creative. However, if students' behaviors stem from their creative personalities, then the self-fulfilled role of *troublemaker* could be changed to something more positive and productive if that energy were channeled toward creative tasks such as improvising and composing.

Of course all students have potential for creative development, and an awareness of creative personality characteristics can help teachers to support and bolster the most positive creative personality traits in students. Music teachers might promote creative potential by offering music tasks or assignments that require some risk taking or even silly behavior, as well as support risk taking and humor in the classroom (when appropriate of course).

Creative Process

The creative process involves the thinking processes that take place as a person is working on a creative product. Because creativity involves an invisible and complex array of factors, there are no exact answers for how this magical "process" takes place. There are, however, several conceptual models of the creative thinking process that have been hypothesized by researchers. Webster developed a model of creative thinking in music (Webster, 1990) that begins with an idea or intention and ends with a creative product. Along this process, one must have support of enabling skills such as musical aptitude, and an environment that supports creative thinking. In this model creativity also requires aesthetic sensitivity and craftsmanship skills, and takes time to move through stages of preparation, incubation, illumination, and verification (borrowed from Wallas, 1926).

Models of the creative process by others point out that personality factors combine with affect, cognitive skills, and creativity relevant skills and highlight the complexity of the process (e.g., Amabile, 1996; Russ, 1996; Sternberg & Lubart, 1991). Perhaps one thing that most agree on is that the creative thinking process requires a combination of both divergent and convergent thinking skills. Divergent thinking is the ability to come up with several possible answers or solutions to a potential problem or stimulus. In music composition, a divergent thinking activity would be to generate several endings to a beginning musical phrase, for example. Convergent thinking is the ability to narrow solutions down to one "right" answer. This is required near the end of the creative thinking process when a product is being fashioned into its final form.

Problem-finding behavior has also been identified as important to the creative thinking process and as an indicative behavior of creative people. *Problem finding* is defined as behavior that includes manipulating, exploring, and selecting elements of a problem, and shaping the parameters of the problem itself. The less that a task is defined, the more that problem-finding behavior is needed. A relationship between problem-finding behavior and creative output has been shown in visual art (e.g., Dillon, 1982; Getzels & Csikszentmihalyi, 1976; Runco, 1994; Runco & Chand, 1995; Sapp, 1997; Wakefield, 1985, 1991, 1994) and in music (Brinkman, 1999; Hickey, 1995). These studies found that subjects who spent more time in exploration of materials before finishing a product produced more creative products than subjects who spent less time exploring.

Sometimes teachers feel the need to take over the problem-finding role and select all of the parameters for a given music project in order to get to a completed product as quickly as possible. With the typical time constraints in music classes today, this is not surprising. However, if the value of music composition lies, at least partly, in the idea that it may promote creative musical thinking, then more time needs to be dedicated to problem-finding and exploratory activities.

In order to stimulate problem finding and creative thinking, open-ended and heuristic tasks (versus contrived and "right-answer" exercises) are needed. The ability to deal with fewer parameters is not only a trait that will encourage more creative thinking, but it is also a trait that needs to be developed in students (especially given the high-stakes testing atmosphere of schools in recent decades). Ideas for these kinds of tasks are provided in the activities outlined at the end of chapters 3 through 7.

Creative Place

The process of creative thinking takes time and is messy, yet our often controlled and hurry-up classroom culture makes it difficult to do this. It is important to encourage and facilitate more careful and thoughtful approaches to creative musical growth in the classroom by providing more time and opportunities to explore a variety of sounds and composition possibilities. Depth over breadth and quality over quantity should be the rule rather than the exception in music composition in order to promote musical creative thinking.

Supporting the creative thinking process through music composition does not need to be as open and uncontrolled as it may seem at this point, however. One can offer guidance for exploration such as asking students to spend time exploring high/low, loud/soft, fast/slow, and different timbres. What are their favorites? Why? Ask students to keep a log of favorite sounds and their descriptions. Listen to recordings of a wide variety of music from traditional as well as nontraditional sound sources. Our ultimate goal should be to get students to become critical listeners as well as creative music explorers on their own. To do this, we need to imbed creative and exploratory activities such as music composition and improvisation into the daily music classroom instruction.

Music composition will nurture creative thinking when exploratory processes such as divergent thinking and problem finding are encouraged in the classroom. By offering more opportunities for exploring in sound through music composition, the creative musical abilities of students will shine. With more creative music composition exercises added to music curricula, there are more opportunities for students to exercise their creative music imaginations and creative personalities. Through music composition, the *creative intelligence* can be stimulated and nurtured in music classrooms and studios. Naturally the varying personalities and temperaments of students promise varying thresholds for the open creative process. But too often it is assumed that students are able to work only within the strictest parameters and that giving fewer parameters means a loss of teacher control. Neither extreme is educational or conducive to creativity. Students need structure and discipline as well as the chance for freedom, spontaneity, and time for exploration and manipulation of musical sounds. We need to provide varied opportunities for students in music composition tasks if we want to encourage and nurture the most creative musical thinking processes. The music composition exercises in chapters 3 through 7 will help to stimulate creative musical thinking through guided divergent activities.

Composing for "Real"

My passion for teaching music composition to children, and my experiences in doing so, has, at times, made me feel self-conscious around "real" composers because I have had no

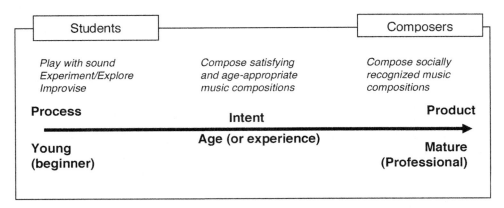

FIGURE 1.1 Continuum of Compositional Experiences

formal education in music composition and I have not composed professionally, much less seriously. How could I possibly teach something that I've never been trained to do (a question most likely asked by many teachers facing this challenge)? This seeming contradiction between what I say and what I do prompted several discussions about music composition with colleague composers and has led me to develop the view that music composition for our students is mostly about a process (rather than the product) that contributes to creative and musical intellectual growth. For professional composers, music composition is more about developing a product using the tools and experiences they have developed (through disciplined study) over the years. In other words, music composition is an activity that has different meanings and/or purposes depending upon where it falls along a continuum of intent and experience.

In figure 1.1, I provide a continuum that represents the different approaches to music composition for young beginners—the typical students in our classrooms—and professional composers. The early level of playing with sound and experimenting can lead to very satisfying music compositions for all of our students. Some students may wish to go further and pursue more advanced composition whereby they become composers, who compose music for a living and are recognized in a social and historical context as professional.

Music composition in school, especially in the beginning stages, might best be viewed as a process-oriented *tool* for teaching and nurturing music exploration skills that will enhance musical understanding as well as musical creative thinking. Teaching music composition at this beginning level also provides scaffolding for the eventual skill of crafting a fine music composition; this should certainly be a goal as students progress through experiences with music composition. For young children (or first-time composers), music composition presents an opportunity to develop a deeper understanding about music through exploration. It is important for teachers to keep in mind that the enjoyment of the process is more important than crafting a product that is "correct." For students in the beginning stages, "It is the exploration itself that motivates rather than the outcome" (Runco, 1996, p. 7). Young children naturally enjoy musical composition because music exploration and process orientation is so natural for them.[5] This is not to say that young students (or novice composers of any age) are incapable of creating authentic musical compositions. Children are capable, and in fact do compose, as has been documented by several researchers (Barrett, 1996; Davies, 1986, 1992, 1994; Marsh, 1995; Moorhead & Pond, 1978/1951; Upitis, 1990, 1992). The point is that children's compositions will likely not be recognized as master-pieces, and may not even sound "right" to our conservatory trained ears. But to compose music is as natural as finger painting, and in the beginning stages, at least, teaching this requires no specialized education, but only the capability to offer materials, time, and support.

The creation of music also provides an important vehicle for the development of one's feelings, emotions, and self-concept. And this development does not need to depend upon technical training. Lowenfeld and Brittain (1987) emphasize this point in their discussion of the importance of creation in visual art that can readily be applied to the "scribbling" involved in the creation of music:

> There is great satisfaction in expressing one's own feelings and emotions in art. Even the very young child who knows nothing about the technical difficulties in pencil rendering, or the various gradations of graphite hardness, can get great satisfaction from making a scribble with a soft pencil. The child expresses self-importance through scribbling, and the satisfaction derived from this achievement is self-evident. The self-confidence that can develop from this type of expression provides the basis for more advanced levels of art. (p. 18)

Natural mental and musical development, along with experiences in music composition activities, will produce natural growth toward product orientation. Some students will pursue music composition as a vocation or avocation and will follow, with our guidance, the necessary and traditional educational path to reach their goals. As students develop and pursue more specialized (product-oriented) composing, it is the obligation of their teachers to find experts capable of giving continued education, just as we might pass our gifted bassoon student on to a professional bassoonist for more specialized tutoring after they outgrow our musical guidance (especially if we have never been trained on the bassoon). All students need the opportunity to reach this point and, at the least, learn to compose and experience music, as shown in the beginning and intermediate stages of the continuum in figure 1.1.

With the traditional music education that music teachers receive (and as I have received), they should have no trouble guiding students through the beginning and intermediate stages of this continuum, to a point where their students are composing satisfying and age-appropriate musical compositions.

Conclusions

For too long, music composition has been put on a pedestal and viewed as a special skill that only an elite few could do. It is time to dispel that notion and offer classroom and studio teachers not only reasons for making music composition an integral part of their curriculum, but also provide practical ideas and activities for doing so.

In this first chapter I have provided a rationale for teachers to begin composition activities in their own classrooms, as well as some thoughts about the creative musical person and process. I have also explored the continuum—as opposed to the gap—that exists from the beginning stages of music exploration to the achievement of professional composition and argued that music teachers are sufficiently educated (even without music composition lessons) to take students along this path toward composing satisfying musical compositions.

In chapter 2 I address some of the stickier issues that plague teaching music composition in schools, such as assessment, notation, and technology. I also introduce a potential curricular model for teaching composition that frames the organization for the remaining chapters. In chapters 3 through 7, I provide readers with an array of composition activities based on the curriculum unit focus for each chapter. Although this book is not just a "how-to" text for music composition, it contains a collection of practical ideas for teachers to use to encourage musical and creative growth through music composition. The composition activities in the middle chapters provide a jumping-off point for music teachers to exercise their own creative thinking and create music composition activities that are customized to their classes and needs (and perhaps to stimulate a few teachers to begin composing themselves!). I argue in the final chapter of this book that because music composition is so musically and educationally multifaceted, it should be placed at the core of the school music curriculum.

The Issues

We must heed Wittgenstein's warning that rules of grammar do not explain
how people speak, nor "cause" them to speak in a certain way.
> J. W. Astington and D. R. Olson, *"The Cognitive Revolution in
> Children's Understanding of Mind"*

If you asked me to diagram a sentence, I'd be hard pressed to do it. I have always struggled with this exercise, and really never grasped the idea of a "dangling participle." Yet I like to think that I write pretty well. The rules of grammar certainly help (and they must have influenced me in a positive way), yet we needn't let rules get in the way of flow and creativity. Music instruction in schools sometimes includes too much focus on grammar and little room for creativity. If we want children to read better, we should have them write stories; if we want children to become poets, we should ask them to write poetry. Similarly, if we want our students to be fulfilled and creative musicians, then they must be given many chances to compose—without the rules of "grammar" impeding their way. We simply need to let them compose and improvise. Creative activities will open the door to a much deeper understanding of all of the concepts, the "rules" that should be taught in music education.

But how can we teach both creativity and the rules of music? Before delving into the main focus of this book, which is to provide activities and ideas for teaching music composition to students, I will address a number of issues that often cloud progress toward teaching music composition in schools. In this chapter, the issues that are examined include composition settings and parameters, notation, use of technology, assessment, and composing in performance ensembles. These issues were chosen because they repeatedly emerge in my conversations with teachers and composers when talking about teaching composition to students, and they also affect the relative success or failure of such endeavors. I do not presume to offer simple solutions, but hope to clarify important points and provide some answers to questions regarding these issues in the succeeding paragraphs.

Composition Settings and Parameters

There are many possible variables from which to choose when developing music composition assignments for students. The environment we create is absolutely crucial for making or breaking our students' comfort with music composition. Some of the choices made can also affect the creative quality and/or success of their compositions. The factors that affect the composition environment, such as open versus closed assignments, time, and group versus individual work, will be examined in this section.

Open versus Closed Composition Assignments

One way to organize types of composition assignments is on a continuum from very closed, with many parameters delineated, to very open, in which the assignments are more "free," with few, if any, teacher parameters (see figure 2.1). Often the "safest" way to begin, particularly in first composition assignments, is to structure closed assignments with very strict parameters in order to control the outcome. When one sets up a careful manuscript template with rules for the durations, note names, time signature, number of measures, and beginning and ending notes, the chance for success at simple and *tonal* music (which is often assumed to be "good") is very high. However, these closed assignments offer little room for exploration and imagination, much less error. Although the intent is understandable, I suggest that teachers try just the opposite in their first and subsequent music composition assignments. That is, they should offer more open assignments with fewer parameters in the beginning stages in order to give students the chance to explore and create music within their own boundaries.

Research studies of creative thinking in music have shown consistently that more creative children feel comfortable exploring many options of sounds before closure when confronted with creative tasks (DeLorenzo, 1989; Hickey, 1995; Levi, 1991; Moorhead & Pond, 1978/1942). Early opportunities for sound exploration and manipulation in the composition process should be made available in the music classroom in order to help students begin to develop their creative music composition repertoire. Activities that involve brainstorming solutions to musical problems, and that do not require one single right answer (such as creating several endings for the beginning of a musical phrase), should be the norm rather than the exception. When given a composition assignment with more leeway to explore, students will be better able to exercise their musical creativity and natural musical curiosity. In other words, more emphasis should be placed on creative process and exploration than finding the "right answer." It is important to point out that giving more open-ended assignments does not mean creating a "free-for-all" classroom culture. Students

Closed	**Assignment Parameters:**	Open
Evaluative	**Assessment Type:**	Non-evaluative feedback

FIGURE 2.1 Open and Closed Assignment Continuum

need control and need to know their boundaries, so although more open assignments allow for more creative music compositions, students must still understand the importance of working without disturbing others and following rules for time limits or getting assignments finished, and so forth.

However the point is not to exclude closed assignments altogether. There are clear circumstances in which giving a very specific assignment is most appropriate. One of the most useful purposes for giving a closed composition assignment is to teach a musical concept. When students are learning a new musical concept, I would argue that the quickest way for them to learn (and for the teacher to assess their understanding) is through music composition. For example, say we want to introduce the concept of sixteenth notes to a class of students. The most creative approach to assess whether students understand the lesson, and the way for teachers to apply the lesson creatively, is to construct a relatively closed composition assignment that requires use of sixteenth notes. A template that includes the measures, time signature, and beginning and ending notes will help the students to get started and be able to concentrate on using sixteenth notes in their compositions—which is the intent of the lesson. In this case the parameters are carefully delineated so that students can compose music, yet at the same time allow the teacher to assess their understanding of the concept being taught and give students a chance to apply their knowledge at level of complexity that is more authentic than simply providing an answer on a paper-and-pencil test. And when students complete their sixteenth-note composition, it will be immediately clear whether they understand the concept of sixteenth notes.

The issue of open versus closed assignments is inextricably linked to the assessment issue. If the purpose of a composition assignment is specific (i.e., to teach how to write in rondo form), or is to teach a concept (such as in the sixteenth-note example), then the assignment can and should be evaluated for quality. If a composition assignment is open, however, then simple feedback would be more appropriate than a qualitative evaluation. Nonevaluative feedback given on an open assignment is more helpful (and fairer) than giving an evaluation such as a grade. Imagine how anxious students would feel if they were asked to compose a piece of music, with no other guidelines except that it be something good, knowing that it will be graded. This is not only unfair to students, but also difficult to do! On the other hand, if the assignment is to write an 8-measure composition in 6/8 time using eighth, quarter, and dotted-quarter notes, it would be easy to evaluate students' understanding of, and their ability to write using these parameters. Giving a grade on such a "closed" type of assignment makes perfect sense. Figure 2.1 shows the types of assignments and assessment types described above.

Researchers have found an interesting interaction between the parameters and assessment method of an assignment and the effects on creativity and intrinsic motivation.[1] Folger, Rosenfield, and Hays (1976) discovered an inconsistency in literature related to effects of extrinsic motivation on creativity: specifically, the overjustification hypothesis that stated that external reward had a detrimental effect upon intrinsic motivation. They found that the variable of choice in a given task mediates motivation: a positive relationship exists

TABLE 2.1 **The interaction between instructional set and levels of external reward and its effect upon creative output and intrinsic motivation**

	Instructional Set	
Reward	Closed (Informed) Task	Open Task
Low External Reward	Low creativity	High creativity
	High intrinsic motivation	High intrinsic motivation
High External Reward	High creativity	Low creativity
	Low intrinsic motivation	Low intrinsic motivation

between external reward and intrinsic motivation under conditions in which little choice is given in the task, whereas an inverse relationship exists between external reward and intrinsic motivation under high-choice conditions (Eisenberger & Cameron, 1998). The type of choice conditions related to a given task, then, must qualify the overjustification hypothesis.

Amabile (1979, 1996) also discovered that when subjects were given rewards for completing certain creative tasks, they indeed showed more creativity. This contradicted a previous theory that nonrewarded tasks produced more creative products. The purpose of her 1979 study was to reconcile these contradictory findings by identifying the instructional sets under which extrinsic rewards might undermine creativity, and those that might enhance it. The results showed that the evaluated (high external reward) groups scored significantly lower on creative scores of their visual art products than the nonevaluated (low external reward) groups *except* when explicit instructions (closed task) were given for creating a product. Though this group (closed task and evaluation) scored highest of all on creativity, they scored lowest in interest of the required task. The group whose task was open and without evaluation (open task, low external reward) exhibited a high level of intrinsic interest to match its high level of creativity. This finding was in agreement with others (Eisenberger & Cameron, 1998; Folger et al., 1976), in that the conditions of the task will mediate the effect of external reward on intrinsic motivation and creative output. This interaction between instructional sets and types of reward and its effect upon motivation and creativity is illustrated in table 2.1[2]. (More specific ideas for approaches to assessment are provided later in this chapter.)

The ideal condition then, for supporting high intrinsic motivation and high creative output is one in which individuals perceive that external rewards are low, and the tasks involved are relatively open (i.e., the upper right-hand cell in table 2.1). Of course, the formula in table 2.1 is only a theory, and the realities of teaching are complex: many tacit factors confound the issue of assignment parameters, assessment, intrinsic motivation, and creativity. Students come to the classroom with a multitude of personality traits that may inhibit or contribute to their creative and motivational approach toward learning, and therefore they also approach composing through different "pathways" (Burnard & Younker, 2004). Different students have varying thresholds for ambiguity: some students will have an easier time with strict parameters, whereas others will prefer the freedom of few parameters. We also know that setting up closed assignments is necessary for achieving specific teaching goals. Too much of either extreme for too long is not the best educational practice. Making sure that we include a variety of both open and closed (and in between) parameters, and gear music composition toward problem-based activities in a supportive environment is the best solution.

Time

The development of quality and creative musical ideas takes time. Schools are set up such that teachers must work on a strict and limited time schedule, with few precious moments allowed in a week for music instruction, along with the additional burden of having to produce stellar concerts for public performance. Unfortunately, this hectic approach to teaching may be least conducive for creative thinking. Researchers have provided evidence that when given shorter time to work on a creative task, subjects produced lower scores on fluency, flexibility, and originality tests (Borland, 1988; Morse, Morse, & Johns, 2001). Additionally, researchers found that students produce their most original ideas later in creative tasks rather than earlier (Johns, Morse, & Morse, 2001). My own experience teaching composition to children provides anecdotal evidence to support the notion that they need (and often covet) a significant amount of undisturbed time when composing. I often have had a difficult time convincing students to take a break, even after hours of working on a music composition project.

For the development of quality musical thinking skills through music composition, depth is more important than breadth. Because time for exploration, incubation, and just messing around with musical ideas is conducive to creativity, it is suggested that if only a few class periods can be devoted to music composition in an academic year, these few classes focus on only one musical composition problem, rather than several. Another alternative is to visit a single composition project for a few minutes of each class period and take this time for an entire year rather than offer several small and miscellaneous composition activities.

A more radical thought, as the final chapter in this book suggests, is to focus an entire music curriculum around the original musical compositions of the students in our classrooms, rather than performing, listening to, and analyzing already published music. All of the basic skills that are covered in music class could still be covered using student compositions, and at the same time, students would get the opportunity to compose the music. The time students spend creating and thinking about their own music will reap benefits of musical knowledge beyond the traditional approach of teaching through precomposed (sometimes contrived) musical examples. Chapter 8 will expand on these ideas.

Group and Individual Approaches

Several studies have examined the efficacy and dynamics of group musical composition processes (Claire, 1993/1994; Kaschub, 1997; MacDonald & Miell, 2000; Wiggins, 1994,

2000, 2003) and group creativity processes (Mumford, Feldman, Hein, & Nagao, 2001; Sawyer, 2006). This research shows, as might be expected, that individual composition and group composition require different approaches. Although there is no apparent advantage or disadvantage between teaching musical composition in groups or to individuals, at most times in a classroom setting group composition may be the most convenient and economical approach. Composing in groups requires careful organization, however, and a sensitivity to group dynamics in order to keep all students qualitatively involved in creative musical thinking processes. Just as in any group work, leaders and followers will emerge and a sensitive teacher will arrange and rearrange groups until the right chemistry supports the best dynamics for creative development and learning.

It is also important to allow individual work on music composition. Students use different types of skills in group versus individual situations—skills that are important for music as well as social growth and development. Just as we wish for students to learn to perform as soloists, we also should strive to have students learn to compose music on their own. A healthy variety of both group music composition projects along with individual work is the best solution. The majority of the composition activities that are provided in the following chapters can be accomplished through either individual or group work.

The environment for music composition should be challenging, respectful, fun, and attractive to the curiosity of the learner. Setting up the composition parameters, such as the type of assignment, time given, and group or individual activities, must be carefully choreographed by a skillful and sensitive teacher. The individual differences of students will demand an environment that is adaptable enough to entice even the most finicky learner to produce his/her creative best.

Notation

Although the debate over rote versus note teaching has swung back and forth over the years (Keene, 1982), and between pedagogies (e.g. Orff-Schulwerk, Kodály, Suzuki), the issue of whether or not to teach music notation has not wavered. Regardless of which side of the note/rote debate one is on, when it comes to teaching music, most have agreed that an eventual understanding of traditional music notation is critical for a complete music education. In other words, the debate has not been about *if*, but *when* and with how much emphasis notation should be taught for music reading. There is in fact quite a strong focus on deciphering traditional music notation in American music education that may be partly due to the heavy emphasis we place on music performance in the school music programs.

When I suggest to preservice and in-service teachers that music notation need not be the focus, much less a component of music composition, I find myself up against a deeply ingrained assumption that music notation is not only key to music learning, but central to music composition. Because of this assumption, common mistakes in teaching music composition are to wait to introduce composition until students understand standard notation, or to have students compose only what they are able to notate in standard notation. This would be equivalent to (and as absurd as) not allowing children to make up stories unt they are able to write them down. Children are natural storytellers and music makers long before they acquire formal knowledge of the abstract symbol systems we use to record these products. As Upitis (1992) points out, "Children view themselves as writers long before they view themselves as readers" (p. 53). Her meaning of *writing* in this instance connotes the ability to make things up and produce notation of any sort that is meaningful to the child (certainly nonstandard, and often nondecipherable to adult readers). We should not squelch this proclivity toward creating by first requiring the understanding of a very abstract symbol system that serves only as a convenient record of musical ideas.

Music notation is not music. Music is sound, and notation provides a means for representing that sound, mostly for the purpose of re-creation by others. When we want another person to perform music we've composed, then standard notation might be the most efficient means of doing so. For many cultures (and, I would argue, some ages and experience levels), notation is not the most efficient means for passing on music—imitation is. Though the comprehension of standard music notation should be an eventual goal of our music curricula, it should not be a barrier to teaching music composition. Students should learn to read notation so that they may learn to decipher, in print, other's music, just as they should eventually learn to write standard notation so that they may offer their original music for others to read.[2] However, music notation in the context of composing music should be thought of as only a vehicle that composers use to share their music so that others may perform it. Music notation is neither a prerequisite nor requisite for music composition.

Begin with Students' Notations

"In order to understand formal symbol systems, individuals must first construct their own versions of symbol systems" (Upitis, 1992, p. 10). Children and nontrained adults' ability to understand and decipher standard notation is developmental (Bamberger, 1991; Davidson & Scripp, 1988; Upitis, 1992). That is, they go through stages of understanding notation from simple and nonabstract (graphic) to the abstract symbol system that we use in our traditional notation. The development of this understanding seems to be based on experience rather than age. If we attempt to force the learning of, and use of, a symbol system that is abstract (such as our traditional notation system) too early in the development process, it will cause only confusion, or at least meaningless rote learning. Therefore the first step toward standard notation understanding is allowing students to make up their own notation— often termed *invented notation*. Children (and adults!) learn quickly that notation of *any* kind is helpful for keeping track of what one composes, and they enjoy using their own graphic systems to notate their musical ideas. When students eventually see the need to notate in standard notation for their music composition projects, they will want to learn how to do so, and experience in creating their own notation systems will aid this learning process.

If students have not been exposed to traditional music reading/writing lessons, on first attempts at music composition they will feel most comfortable notating musical ideas using whatever system—graphic, numeric, alphabetic, and so forth—is most meaningful to them. The system they use to write down and keep track of their compositional ideas does not matter. What matters more in music education is that students eventually come to realize the need for standard notation as they simultaneously refine their own systems. Music composition is the best activity to develop this "need to know." Encouraging students to share their original notations with one another will develop in them a tolerance of notational forms different from their own and at the same time stimulate a real curiosity about standard notation as they refine their own systems. Ask students to compose music that they must teach to the class or a classmate using their notation. When they are developmentally ready and sufficiently curious or motivated, they will begin to learn to read and write standard music notation (and discover, in many cases, that it is a pretty efficient system). In the meantime, students should be encouraged to simply write down their music in any way they want, so that they can remember it, or so that they can teach it to others. If there is no reason to remember it, or no plan to teach the composition to somebody else, it does not matter if the composition is notated.[3]

Using Ears Rather than Eyes

I often start music composition activities with students by using computer sequencing software and turn off any notation feature of the software. This forces students to use their ears more than their eyes while exploring and organizing sounds into original music compositions, allowing them to more wholly enjoy their creative musical task. The computer software takes care of the recording, notating, and remembering for them. I have only once encountered a child who was reluctant to compose in this way. The following scenario is shared because it offers a description of this instance when a child preferred to use standard notation. It is the only time that this occurred in my teaching, yet it offers a possible scenario for teachers.

Sam

On the first day of the four-Saturday music composition workshop, I took the fourth- and fifth-grade students to the computer lab, each at his/her own computer, and asked them to explore the available synthesizer sounds as well as become familiar with the sequencing software by recording some musical ideas. They quickly learned to record music they played on the keyboard into multiple tracks and had the option of using any of 128 general MIDI sounds. The first assignment I gave was to compose a "musical scenery"—that is, compose a song that described a particular setting (forest, subway, lunchroom, outer space, etc.). They were asked to use at least four tracks simultaneously but could use any of the timbres they wished. The goals of this first assignment were to give the students the opportunity to explore different sounds, to learn the software, and to be immediately successful with a first music composition. The graphic notation option (as opposed to standard notation) appeared on the screen to encourage them simply to explore and record sound manipulation—and not to worry about reading notes.

One student, Sam, was immediately confused with the assignment and situation. He did not do anything for a long time but sat and stared at the computer screen. When asked what was wrong, Sam stated that he did not know how to play the piano and wondered if he could compose a song using "real notes" instead (standard notation on the screen would allow him to "point and click" each note into the program rather than play it in from the synthesizer/keyboard). However, the software program was a sequencing program, as opposed to a notation program, and therefore not conducive to easy point-and-click notation—that would be too clumsy and would surely cause Sam more undue frustration. An immediate decision had to be made: do I open a notation program for Sam, so that his first computer composition project is notated in standard notation as he wished? Or do I gently coerce Sam into forgetting about standard notation, to use his ears, and simply experiment and record something, *anything*, using the keyboard? I chose to go with the latter option. Sam was a sport and pleasantly shrugged his shoulders with a *whatever* attitude and went to work. A few minutes later, watching from afar, I could see that Sam seemed to be enthusiastically playing with the sounds on the keyboard/synthesizer. When he caught my eye, he beckoned me over excitedly: "Listen to what I recorded! " My first hearing revealed what sounded like a messy conglomerate of several different timbres playing all at once, and then slowly fading away. "Interesting, Sam! Tell me about it." "It's the *Mission Impossible* theme," he replied. I listened again, and sure enough, deep within the tangle of sounds, I could faintly recognize the *Mission Impossible* theme song. Sam had used his ear to sound it out and record it into one of the tracks. Then around that he added the wild sounds of which he was so enthusiastically proud.

The incident with Sam illustrates several points. First, although Sam was reluctant, with gentle persuasion he agreed to at least try composing outside of the comfort zone of what he knew best: standard notation. Once he overcame this hurdle, he never looked back. Second, this persuasion to get Sam to ignore his eye for notation illustrated how he really used his ears to come up with a familiar tune while playing around on the keyboard. Music composition, more than any other music activity, requires the most "ear work" because of the aural decisions that must be made in order to organize sounds into some acceptable form. When we add the "eye" distraction, that is, trying to notate on paper what we hear or wish to hear, we create a barrier to music composition—at least in the beginning stages. Composing music requires careful and creative organization of aural sounds, whereas notating is a secondary component. I have had several students without any piano background show a remarkable ability to re-create songs they knew by ear on the keyboard. They then enjoyed "dressing them up" with accompaniments of different timbres and rhythms, and so forth. Indeed, sometimes more complex music, such as that created by young children as well as contemporary composers, is more conducive to nontraditional notation than standard notation. Of course a long-term goal for composers should be to learn to write what they hear so that others can play their music through our standard notation system. However, this should not be the first step toward teaching music composition.

So, as teachers begin to experiment incorporating music composition activities into their classrooms, I would strongly suggest that they begin without the barrier of standard notation. Notation will develop as it is needed and/or through other music classroom learning activities. It should not stand in the way of composing music.

Technology

"Musical creativity owes much to inventions" (Arieti, 1976, p. 239), and the invention of the computer has spawned tremendous new possibilities for music and music making. Computer technology is to music composition in the classroom what the phonograph was to music appreciation just after the turn of the twentieth century. Computer technology is a tool that can transform the way we teach and the way students learn music. It opens as many avenues to music composition for our students as the phonograph did for music listening. As educational technology guru Seymour Papert proclaims, "The computer breaks down the barriers that traditionally separate the preletterate from the letterate, the concrete from the abstract, the bodily from the disembodied" (1993, p. 49).[4]

Computer music sequencing and notation software,[5] along with a keyboard/synthesizer or other input device, provides learners with a large and varied palette of sounds, from traditional orchestral instruments to popular instruments to an array of synthesized sounds. The computer allows users to record and store several ideas at once, and these ideas can then be varied by pitch, rhythm, duration, timbre, volume, and more. Most significant is that any recorded idea can be accessed and played back immediately. One no longer has to wait to have music performed by live humans in order to get feedback on how it sounds. The computer music workstation provides an entire recording studio at the fingertips of the young composer![6]

A New Music Literacy

Another compelling reason for promoting the use of technology in composition activities has to do with the new kind of music and music making that relies solely on computer technology. This new music literacy is one that our students are learning outside of, and in spite of, the teaching that takes place in our music classrooms. As teachers, we must somehow connect this new literacy with the "letteracy" that is part of our traditional music classrooms.

Music technology not only offers more flexible accompaniment, listening, recording, and music instruction tools for teaching, but there are now new approaches to composition and improvisation that emulate musical styles in popular culture. The growing collection of new mixing software imitates approaches to music making by DJs and hip hop artists by providing tools for mixing (vertically or horizontally) rhythmic sound samples. Software programs such as Groovemaker, Mixman, GarageBand, and Virtual DeeJay provide the user (composer) with tools to mix digital music files and add layers of pulsating rhythmic tracks and "bass tracks" to create completely new compositions. The new *remix* approach to composition using computer technology is described in the manual for the software Mixman:

> In recent years there has been a significant amount of hype about electronic music, remixes, and DJ culture. Record companies have always remixed versions of songs to breathe new life into them or make them appeal to a specific music market. A slow ballad might be turned into a stylish dance song. But what is a remix? A remix in its truest sense is the art of taking elements from an existing song and adding new musical elements in order to augment or change the feel of the original song. It is quite common today to find artists that alter the original parts of a song to the point at which the line between remixing and composing is significantly blurred. As we approach the new millennium, with software like *Mixman Studio,* the definition of DJ, artist, remixer and producer will continue to change and grow. (*Mixman Studio Manual*, p. 3-2)

Looping software (software that allows users to pick from predigitized sounds that can be looped and pasted into layers of tracks) is the most recent type of technology available for music composition. A quick critique from traditionalists may dismiss this software as being too easy to turn out rapid or thoughtless compositions. Yet, to do it well—that is, to create musically expressive compositions—is incredibly difficult for those of us accustomed to thinking about music composition in more traditional ways.

I use computer software and keyboard/synthesizers early and often when I teach music composition to children and adults. I do not believe it is absolutely necessary, nor even the panacea for teaching music composition, but I use computer technology whenever I have the access because of the extra tools it offers me as a teacher. Computer technology provides a new and exciting avenue of possibilities for opening up the music composition world to students who are becoming increasingly more computer literate. However, I do not use it exclusively, nor do I recommend using it exclusively (especially in the beginning stages). I vary all music composition activities between the use of computer technology and the use of traditional (and nontraditional) classroom techniques in order to expose learners to the possibilities of music making in any circumstance. Students will figure out how to use it and may find the new "literacy" more appealing to their learning styles and more relevant to their personal cultures. Ideas for music composition technology assignments will be shared in each of the activity chapters that follow.

Assessment

One of the most important yet confounding issues that teachers face when dealing with music composition in the classroom is that of assessment. Unlike a musical performance, which is relatively easy to rate in an objective manner, it is difficult to deal objectively with the subjective art of music composition. Musical performances have, of course, some leeway in expressive interpretation, but are mainly judged based on the performer getting the correct notes, rhythms, key signatures, and so forth. We also have a fairly reliable set of benchmarks for knowing at what level and capability performers should be for each year of their experience on an instrument. Because of the lack of music composition teaching in the schools, there are no benchmark data to aid teachers in assessing the relative success or failure of students' music compositions at different grade or experience levels.

For some, there are the questions of not only how to judge subjective work of children, but whether one should judge at all. Viktor Lowenfeld, an influential art educator, philosopher, and researcher, took a nonnegotiable stance against evaluation of students' visual art in the context of the art classroom:

> There should be one place in the school system where marks do not count. The art room should be a sanctuary against school regulations, where youngsters are free to be themselves and to put down their ideas and feelings and emotions without censorship, where they can evaluate their own progress toward their own goals without the imposition of an arbitrary grading system. (Lowenfeld & Brittain, 1987, p. 176)

One can easily imagine how this stance in visual art could parallel beliefs about evaluating music composition, since a child's original visual art is similar in its subjectivity to a child's original music. As discussed earlier, we know that intrinsic motivation and its role in creativity presents a complex array of factors involved in establishing the most conducive environments for creative output. One finding seems consistent, however: giving a reward for a task (such as a grade) has the potential to be detrimental to the intrinsic motivation for the task (Deci, Koestner, & Ryan, 2001; Kohn, 1993) as well as the creativity of the resulting product (Amabile, 1996; Hennessey, 2000; Hennessey & Amabile, 1988). Lowenfeld's aversion toward evaluating children's art may be fair, and the lesson may be that teachers who want to encourage the most creative output from their students should try to avoid always giving rewards or evaluative marks for creative work.

On the other hand, it is probably not wise to quickly and simply dismiss assessment of music composition because of its subjectivity. Assessment comes in many forms and can aid in the learning process. It can be a nod of approval, a scathing critique, honest feedback, an evaluative mark such as a grade or a simple reward for a job well done. Whatever form we use, it must be used carefully because of the subjective and personal nature of music composition.

When I first began working with children on music compositions, I often wondered about the "quality" of the compositions. It seemed random and scattered to me. But with patience and experience, I eventually learned that my aesthetic and theirs were not only different, but that we could mutually learn from each other. I also learned that the development of "quality" in a music composition is a long, slow process. I have learned to not judge quickly when I hear a child's musical composition. Rather, I ask questions to learn more about their intent. This questioning critique (as opposed to a telling critique), when done by themselves, their peers, and me will help students develop abilities as lifelong critical thinkers and self-assessors. We have much to learn in this area and might begin by examining the work of our peers in visual arts and creative writing (e.g., Calkins, Hartman, & White, 2005; Reese, 2003; Soep, 1996).

So, rather than dismiss the notion of assessment of music composition altogether, I hope to offer ideas for teachers who are faced with giving feedback on their students' music compositions. In this discussion I come back to the continuum of feedback presented in figure 2.1 that can range from evaluative (rating the quality either in relation to others or a standard benchmark) to nonevaluative feedback (simply describing what we hear without "good" or "bad" implied). Feedback need not always be evaluative but should provide objective information in order to help students develop their own critical skills and growth as musicians. Students likely realize when the feedback they receive is honest:

> Some compositions are simply not as successful as others, and children know this as well as the adults who teach them. Just as some paintings or stories show more imagination than others, so too do the musical creations of children. It would be a mistake to treat all compositions in the same way, and this is apparent to children as well as to the adults with whom they may share their works. (Upitis, 1992, p. 32)

One reason for the difficulty of assessing musical compositions is that composing music is an inherently subjective act—beauty lies in the ears of different beholders. However, recent research has shown that music teachers *can* come into a reasonable agreement as to what is a good composition and what is not (Bangs, 1992; Brinkman, 1999; Hickey, 1995, 2001). This research on "consensual assessment" shows that given a variety of children's musical compositions, groups of teachers are able to consistently agree as to which compositions are the most creative, most appealing, or most technically solid.[7] This is not to say that teachers need to get a panel of judges together every time they want to assess musical compositions, but I mention it in order to boost teachers' confidence that they indeed have the musical ability to tell a more "successful" composition from another. I often meet teachers who are reluctant to try music composition in their classroom because they feel unprepared to give feedback. Music teachers' musical background and training provides all of the necessary tools for making accurate and thoughtful comments about their students' compositions.

Feedback as Assessment

The most productive first approach to assessment is simple observation of, questioning about, and subsequent reflection on various components of both the compositional process as well as the final product. The first step is to begin with a question to find out what the student intends in his/her music composition. In the process of conferring with students on their creative writing, Calkins (Calkins, Hartman, & White, 2005) labels this first step *research*. "Observe and interview to try to understand what the child is trying to do as a writer. Probe to glean more about the child's intentions" (Calkins et al., p. 7). It is easy for us to leap to conclusions about a child's music composition—often using our conservatory trained ears as benchmarks—when in fact a child may have a completely different idea as to why he or she made a particular musical decision in a composition. Learning of their intention before critiquing shows children that we respect them as composers, and will help us guide the creative process in a much more respectful manner.

Reese (2003) surveyed research on composers and from art and poetry educators to come up with these ideas regarding feedback on artwork:

- Observe carefully, and know students' music well before offering critiques.
- Encourage students to find solutions to musical problems on their own; help them discover how other composers may have addressed problems similar to ones they are having.
- Use a systematic approach to description of the work, and delay interpretation or judgment.
- When changing or adding to a student's music, offer incremental changes based directly on the student's musical ideas.
- Help students who are stuck by varying one of their ideas or by offering incomplete portions of music to extend.
- Validate students' work through genuine responses because these are inherently valuable even when they do not contain detailed comments.
- Use a facilitative approach to help students find their own composing interests in addition to a didactic approach, which gives direct suggestions on changes that could or should be made in the music.

Hickey and Reese (2001) developed a guideline for new teachers for evaluating their assessment of feedback on their students' compositions. The traits of good feedback include the following:

- Positive feedback should be specific to the composition or composition process, rather than general ("empty").
- The critique of any weak areas in the composition should be specific.
- Feedback should include clear analysis/description of the important musical elements of the composition.

- Feedback should provide musical (and/or technical) terms that are appropriate for the age level of the composer.
- Feedback should contain specific suggestions for change if necessary.
- Any suggestions for change should be musically appropriate for the composition.
- Suggestions for change should be appropriate for the age level of the composer.
- The feedback should contain effective devices to communicate imaginatively about suggestions or the piece as a whole, for example humor, metaphors, analogies, expressive language.

Though these suggestions may seem like common sense, they are useful as reminders for providing quality feedback to student composers.

The process that a young creator goes through can be guided and helped along, just as the resulting product can be commented on in relation to others that the child has done. The next step after research is to examine the processes and products of composition. The following paragraphs offer suggestions for providing proper feedback to young composers in both the process stage as well as the final product.

Process Feedback

As in all educational endeavors, and especially in more subjective areas such as visual art, creative writing, or music composition, appraising the process toward a goal can be as enlightening as evaluating the final product. In creative writing, several typologies for the writing process have been developed to aid teachers in stimulating and guiding students' creative products. A useful process typology, applied by Tsisserev (1997) to analyze music composition processes of high school students, was borrowed from the creative writing literature (Hillocks, 1975) and may prove helpful for teachers to use with music compositions (see figure 2.2).

The process categories that Tsisserev applies to music composition are idea generation, idea development/expansion, idea organization, and idea expression. The composer begins by generating his or her ideas, inspired by any myriad of stimuli (including teacher instruction). The "idea" may be a simple short musical motif, or it might be a grand soundscape inspired by a sunset. At this point, a teacher may help by asking questions about

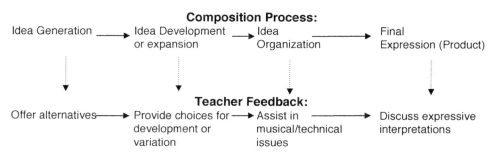

FIGURE 2.2 Music Composition Process Points for Teacher Feedback

potential alternatives such as pictures or stories or colors. The idea then moves on to the next level, where it is expanded upon and developed into longer and more complex ideas. Here, a teacher might aid by asking about students' choices for development or variation, or by prompting the composer to reflect on the development process he or she chooses. The composer then organizes his or her ideas by creating patterns, repeating motifs, transposing, and rearranging into a more complete whole. Students who struggle at this point can be aided by teacher guidance on more technical matters. Finally, the composer applies his or her final touches to a composition in order to help communicate the expressive qualities that are intended. It is at this stage, Tsisserev points out, that the composer relies most on his or her overall musical knowledge and decision-making ability. Teacher awareness of each of these stages of the composition process may help make feedback to student composers most fruitful.

Product Assessment

There are several criteria that one could use when assessing musical compositions. One is to examine the effectiveness of each of the musical elements (e.g., melody, rhythm, texture,). Another is to check the completeness of the assignment task or the appropriateness of the writing for the instrument for which a composition is written. It is also important to consider (and teach young composers to consider) the larger, more general aspects of music composition such as the overall creativeness, craftsmanship, and aesthetic appeal of a final composition. These more general criteria are important in order to show that they are valued, to encourage more holistic and creative thinking, and to keep a sense of artistry in the composition process.

Bringing to light the subjective qualities such as creativity or aesthetic appeal also stimulates healthy discussion among students. For example, why might we call something aesthetically appealing yet not creative? Can an object that is aesthetically appealing be one that we do not like? Can music be creative but not appealing? An awareness of, and ability to reflect upon, these larger qualities of art will lead to more critical musical thought by our students as they develop as composers. One way to highlight the areas of creativity, aesthetic appeal, and craftsmanship in a music composition is through a rubric designed to define these words.

Rubrics

An extremely effective device for offering feedback to students is a rubric. An assessment rubric is a scoring tool that lists criteria or components to be evaluated along with descriptors for each of these components. The descriptors for each component often provide three or four gradient levels of quality that range from *best* to *worst*. The rubric components and their corresponding descriptors should be closely related to the assignment task and therefore unique to each assignment and context. The connection of an assignment to an assessment rubric will not only help students understand the assignment expectations, but it will also clearly inform teachers of students' progress and understanding. So rather than giving a single (and often seemingly subjective and mysterious) grade upon completion of a composition assignment, an assessment rubric should be given *with* a composition assignment so that both teachers and students are aware of the expectations for a successful composition.

The following steps are suggested for setting up composition assignments and corresponding assessment rubrics:

1. Determine the components of the end product that are most important for the objectives of that assignment (e.g., number of measures, use of rhythms, specific tonal center). Delineate three to five of these components for the assessment rubric (too many will feel overwhelming; too few will not provide enough feedback).
2. Write down, as explicitly as possible, those characteristics of each component that are deemed most positive and those characteristics that are the opposite—either by lacking in positive characteristics or because of low quality. These descriptions should be brief and concise.
3. Place these two descriptions at opposite ends of a "quality line."
4. Work to fill in the middle rubric descriptions between the two end points by describing these qualities.

As mentioned previously, a combination of specific components with more general components such as creativeness, craftsmanship, and aesthetic appeal should be used to encourage the latter. A rubric for the following assignment is offered as an example in figure 2.3.

Compose a melody (or rhythm) that is in rondo form. Your "A" theme should be at least 4 measures long. Create at least two other themes. Be sure that you can play or sing your melody, and that it is interesting and something that you like when you are finished. You should revise it as often as necessary until you are satisfied. Your completed composition should be at least 20 measures long.

Peer Assessment

A very powerful means of learning through assessment is allowing opportunities for peer critique. This requires the development of a classroom culture in which listening and peer critique are done thoughtfully and sensitively. Students might have a composing buddy with whom they consistently share, critique and help with each other's compositions. Periodic performance days might be set aside in which student composers perform their compositions, even in rough stages, in order to get helpful feedback from their peers. The use of a simple feedback form for listening to and critiquing peer compositions works well for older students. Teachers can serve as models by composing along with students and asking them for feedback as well. Peer assessment is a powerful learning tool for all involved and is highly recommended for teaching music composition.

	Quality			
Components:	**Needs work**			**Terrific!**
Correct rondo form	No formal structure.	There is a clear 4 measure theme, and one other theme. Not in rondo form, however.		The form of the composition is clearly Rondo form with 2 other themes—ABACA.
Appropriate writing for the instrument	The composition is written outside of the practical range of the instrument it is written for.	The composition is written within the practical range of the instrument. However there are too many difficult passages for this level player.	The composition is written within the practical range of the instrument. Only 1 or 2 technically awkward passages for this level player.	The composition falls within the proper range of the instrument, and is performable for this level of proficiency.
Creativity	This composition is not original (it was composed before).	This composition is original, but does not contain any interesting features.	This composition is original and provides some interest.	This composition is completely original and provides interesting features for the listener.

FIGURE 2.3 **Rubric Sample**

Some General Assessment Guidelines

The more specific we can be with students about what it is we want, the more we can assess whether they get it or not. But we should not formally evaluate or even casually assess everything that our students create. Research on children's creativity supports the notion that intrinsic motivation and creativity can be squelched when the prospect of evaluation is imminent.[8] Therefore music composition should not always be approached as an assignment to be completed and graded, but more as an ongoing activity in which students are given opportunities and time to experiment with the manipulation and organization of musical sound. Students should be encouraged to compose, edit, revise, and doodle with their musical ideas as often as possible and then keep their sketches as well as final compositions in their own personal "portfolios" (much like visual artists keep sketches and drafts). Students should have the opportunity and privacy to compose and keep drafts for nobody's ears but their own. Portfolio organization and assessment may be most conducive to this approach, as students can choose works for teachers to judge and keep works not to be judged.

Assessment, critique, and evaluation of our students' musical compositions need not be a negative or squelching act, but one in which dialogue and learning take place between students and teachers in an ongoing reflective and growing process. The ultimate goal is for our students to be their own best judges of their creative endeavors.

Composing in Ensembles

Are we asking our students to be creative in our band, orchestra, or choir rehearsals? Are we allowing them to "color outside of the lines, and paint by any number they want"? Do we ever let them take charge from the podium? Too often, and for obvious reasons, all of the musical decision-making processes are left up to the conductor. Students who partake in performance ensembles as part of their school music education are rarely asked to make aesthetic or creative musical decisions.

It is essential to understand how the benefits of composition activities can actually enhance students' understanding of music and therefore enrich the overall ensemble experience. Although the following learning opportunities likely can happen while performing and listening to music, composition and improvisation offer rich avenues as well.

Composition and improvisation

- provide authentic and powerful ways to assess student knowledge;
- provide the most direct route to teaching musical concepts;
- provide a powerful means for ear training;
- provide a fun and creative vehicle for teaching notation;
- reveal otherwise untapped talents, often in our least suspected students; and
- provide a unique "way in" and, therefore, deeper understanding of music than would be reached through performing only.

But how can we possibly teach music composition to an unwieldy group of students holding instruments? Starting with beginners, I would suggest that any new concept that is being taught should be composed. Once students learn two notes, ask them to compose a short composition for their instrument using these two notes. The students will likely practice their original compositions more than the music in their method books. As students progress and learn more concepts, have them compose the concepts they are learning (e.g., ask students to compose in 6/8 time when first learning 6/8 time). If working with a large group, collect short compositions, enter them into a computer notation program and transpose for all to play. Warm up by sight reading students' compositions. Students' desire to create music for their peers will be great, and the satisfaction greater than they might get by playing the trite music often presented in beginning instrument books. The ownership that students have invested in the music they write is a natural motivator. Students may also enjoy composing using music notation software.

Once students are no longer beginners and are playing or singing in large ensembles in middle or high school grades, I suggest that teachers create composition activities inspired by the music they are performing. Using the usual analysis for score study, ask the questions, "What about each of these elements lends itself to a composition activity?" and "What compositional technique did the composer use that might be easy for my students to try?" Figure 2.4 provides the types of analysis questions one might ask when going through

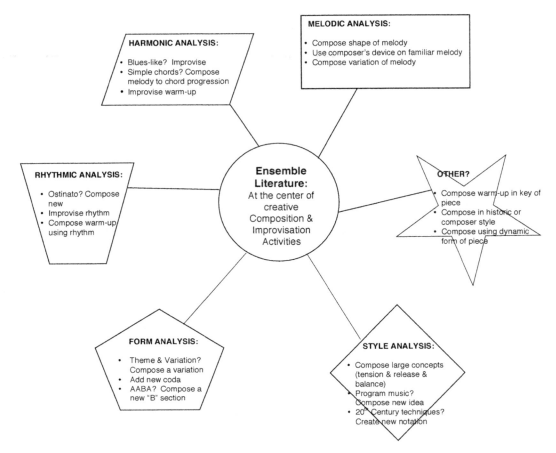

FIGURE 2.4 Compositional Analysis of Ensemble Literature

a score to see if there is anything exceptional about the compositional technique that would be worth trying with the students in order to develop a greater understanding of the score.

It becomes a matter of analyzing the music from the perspective of the composer to see whether there is any device that would work as a compositional tool. This does not work in all ensemble music. However, when one discovers a compositional device to use as an example for a student activity, then it can only enhance the students' musical awareness and appreciation for their ensemble music. Specific lessons for composing in ensemble are included in each of the activities at the end of chapters 3 through 7.

So Where Do We Begin?

I have had so many teachers ask me, "How do you begin to get students to compose?" Although there is no "right" answer, as I've worked with students on music composition over the years, and struggled to find the "perfect" approach for getting students to start composing, I simultaneously read and learned from literature on teaching visual art and creative writing. I came across the sensational work of Lucy McCormick Calkins, who has virtually defined the contemporary "rules" for teaching creative writing to students.[9] I find that her "writing workshop" approach aligns with the principles that work best when teaching "creative writing" in music (music composition) to students.

One of the most helpful ideas from this writing workshop approach tackles the problem of how to start (this is also related to the issue of open versus closed assignment parameters, which was addressed previously). In the writing workshop approach, as well as in my favorite composition texts by Paynter (1992) and Vella (2003), the stimulus for composing begins with a problem. *But whose problem?* is often the question. Should the teacher pose the problem, in the form of a carefully articulated assignment? Or should the problem come from the child? A landmark study of visual artists by Getzels and Csikszentmihalyi in 1976 found that problem finding was a hallmark of the most creative artists. The most creative individuals tend to find the problem themselves; that is, they begin creative projects by choosing what parameters to set for themselves. Whether they're working on a composition, a painting, a play, or a plan for a building, "problem finders" seek to define the problem themselves and then begin to "solve" it.

I have found that asking students to "find the problem" by challenging them to "compose anything you want," tends to paralyze older students who have been trained to follow specific directions given to them by teachers throughout their schooling. Calkins (1983) confirms this notion in her writings about guiding creative writing with children. As teachers, we probably need to provide the "problem" for our students (although if given the chance to compose early and often in their music education, students with creative musical interests may begin composing on their own—finding their own problems—soon after they start to get it), as well as provide freedom for students to define their own.

One of the most motivating types of creative writing or creative music composition prompts is to give students an assignment that allows them to express that which is important to their lives. Therefore, one of the first I assignments I give is to ask students to think of a place that is meaningful to them and then to compose a musical scenery that depicts the sounds (or feelings) in that place. One student decided to compose a song about the police knocking on his neighbors' doors to arrest a murderer in a ghetto of Chicago, whereas another (in the same class of boys) wrote a composition for meditation because he had recently learned about how to meditate when he was angry. Experiment with a variety of prompts, such as those listed in table 2.2, to discover which work best for a particular individual or group of students. Each of these prompts brings to life real situations for students that give them enough freedom to create something that is real to them—something that inspires them.

After starting the process, we might then talk about compositions in terms of form, or I might introduce a new composition prompt that deals with musical form. I then move to the musical elements to help guide and shape the compositional process. After spending some time working on more detailed ideas (even notation perhaps), such as melody or rhythm, I move on to the bigger elements of "unity and variety," "tension and release," and "balance."

TABLE 2.2 Potential Music Composition Prompts

- Compose a musical scenery to depict a place (real or imaginary).
- Compose music to accompany a story (fiction or nonfiction).
- Compose music inspired by a painting (abstract or realistic).
- Compose music that is a signature for your identity.
- Compose music to depict a mood (now or in a specific situation).
- Compose music to depict a color(s) or shape(s).
- Compose music that describes your childhood.

A Composition Curriculum Structure

Figure 2.5 provides a structure that I have found to be successful for initiating and then organizing a flow of composition activities for students. The white arrows show the specific concepts that I follow in order:

1. Define, Listen, and Explore
2. Compositional Prompts (Inspiration and Identity)
3. Form
4. Musical Elements
5. Big Elements

One could move through the sequence in different ways, as long as the "Define, Listen, and Explore" concept is always approached first, followed by the "Composition Prompts." The gray arrows in the structure offer alternative routes to activities once the first two areas are explored.

Regardless of which sequence is used, teaching composition should move through each of these areas in a spiral manner: that is, upon completion of the entire sequence at one skill level, one would begin again and move through the sequence at a more sophisticated level. One cycle through the entire structure could take anywhere from 3 weeks to 4 years, depending upon the amount of time and depth of experiences devoted to music composition in instruction. For example, this structure could provide the basis for a curriculum that spans 3 years in a middle school, or the course of a 1-semester secondary general music class, or repeated several times in spiral fashion over 6 years of an elementary music program.

Each component of the curriculum structure is explained briefly below, and more detail about each section is provided in the subsequent chapters.

Define, Listen and Explore: Chapter 3

At a beginning, general stage, students work to define music and music composition. Exposure to a wide variety of music and developing critical listening skills are important. Students then begin exploring sounds and becoming aware of sounds in the environment.

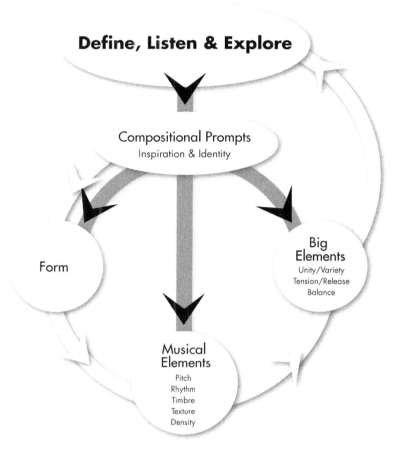

FIGURE 2.5 Composition Curriculum Structure

Composition Prompts: Inspiration and Identity: Chapter 4

What inspires you? How can you channel that into musical form? What musical voice shapes your own identity? Perhaps the greatest reason for creating in the arts is also the greatest motivator and inspiration for getting started: the meaningful events in our daily lives. There is no simpler way to get children composing than to have them create sounds inspired by important people, places, or events in their lives.

Form: Chapter 5

Form is the essence of music and of life. In this section, ideas are shared that help students understand an awareness of form in music by composing in different forms.

Musical Elements: Chapter 6

This section provides more specific and carefully prescribed assignments that focus on the elements we use to describe Western/tonal music, such as melody, harmony, texture, rhythm, and timbre.

Big Elements: Chapter 7

It is the "big" elements of tension/release, unity/variety, and balance that make music interesting. This section focuses on these elements through composition assignments that use them explicitly.

Suggestions for Organization of Composition Activities

The units in the curriculum model were developed based on ideas gleaned from research literature on creative thinking, as well as through my own practice and experience teaching music composition to children. They are offered as guides for teachers to begin to experiment with music composition with their students and perhaps find more effective or relevant steps to follow in their own teaching. I hope that this guide provides more inspiration than prescription!

As students work their way through the organizational scheme and composition exercises, a portfolio routine should be established. Students should be encouraged to keep a collection of all of their musical ideas, as they might collect sketches for a painting or ideas for a story. Musical ideas could be stored in a composition notebook, on a CD, or in a folder on the computer. Periodically ask students to return to their portfolio or collection of previously composed musical ideas to see whether something works for a new assignment. Just as the great composers keep notebooks of musical sketches, so too should children, as a way of observing their own progress and storing musical ideas on which to develop. This also helps establish the attitude that first tries on any compositional assignment do not have to be perfect. The *process* of brainstorming and messing around with many ideas before finding the right one is more important than finding the perfect *product*.

TABLE 2.3 Lesson Activities by Chapter

	Three: Define, Listen and Explore	Four: Composition Prompts: Inspiration and Identity	Five: Form in Music	Six: Musical Elements	Seven: Big Elements
Beginner	Found sound compositions	Who are you?	Same-change-different	Compose a melody	Theme and variation
Intermediate	Sound spaces	Inspired by an event	Beginnings and endings and in between	Applause! Graphic notation	Perform my artwork
Advanced	Prose composition	Memory pages	Song form	Adding harmony to melodies	More with less: minimalism
Technology	Favorite sounds	Sound-scapes	Building blocks	Chord fun	Ostinato
Ensemble	Just scribble!	Exploration etude	SCAMPER	Melody writing for an instrument	Aleatoric music
Other	A listening journal	Arts inspire together	Multimovement composition	Sound textures	Movie soundtrack

The chapters that follow focus on each of the components of the organizational structure shown in figure 2.5. Each chapter begins with discussion about the component and offers ideas for getting students to be more explicitly aware of that component. The second half of each chapter presents sample music composition exercises that apply the chapter focus. There are exercises for beginning, intermediate, and advanced composition levels, music technology, performance ensembles, and "other" miscellaneous composition assignments. It is important to note that *beginning*, *intermediate*, and *advanced* does not apply to grade level, but to composition experience level. The organization and titles of the lesson activities are shown in table 2.3.

The goal of the next five chapters is to provide readers with a variety of ideas for getting students to compose music in various teaching situations through the concepts outlined in the figure 2.5. I hope that these lessons will stimulate hundreds of more ideas for teaching composition in music studios and classrooms.

Define, Listen, and Explore

We are surrounded by all kinds of sounds that are just waiting to be made into music.

JOHN PAYNTER, *Sound and Structure*

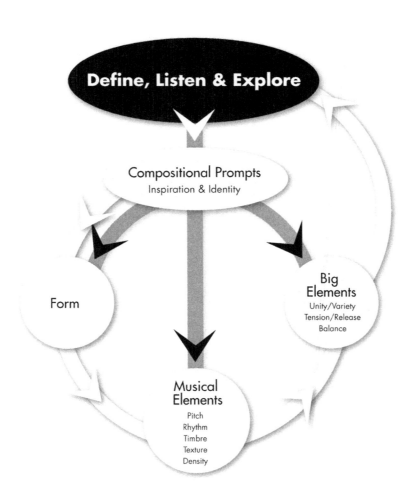

One of the first steps in the process of music composition involves setting the groundwork for musical creativity. This means establishing an open, flexible, and curiosity-supporting atmosphere in the classroom by providing time for exploration of many sounds. And it is at this first stage that I suggest we begin by challenging students with such questions as, what is music? And what does it mean to compose music? Music composition experiences should start with defining, exploring, and listening in order to raise awareness about music and contribute to a solid foundation for composing.

In this chapter I begin by sharing ideas for defining music and music composition, discuss activities for music listening, and conclude with a focus on musical exploration. Although they are presented here sequentially, it is best to think of defining, listening, and exploring as intertwined strands in the first stage of music composition rather than as separate and/or consecutive steps.

Define

What is music? This question often stops students in their tracks, especially when it comes from me, their music teacher. What do you mean, "What is music?" Everybody knows what music is! "Well," I continue to prod, "then what is it?" This question presents a multitude of possible answers and leads to lively classroom debate. It also compels students to focus, often for the first time, on defining the art form in which they are about to create. A secondary benefit of this question is that it allows students to break from their sometimes narrow conceptions about what music really is.

Initially children tend to define music in familiar generic terms, such as "the songs we hear on the radio" or the "songs we learn in music class," or, if related to music theory they have been learning, as the "notes of the scale put together." These are often categories they view as quite distinct. Children consider "music class music" to be in a category different from the "real music" they hear in their everyday life. And, importantly, they think that composing music is something that only a few exceptional (often long dead) individuals do (or did). Music and its creation, when viewed in this limited sense, seem far removed from children's ordinary worlds and especially from their potential identity as composers.

This narrow view of music and composing becomes more entrenched as children progress through music education programs that emphasize note reading and/or performance, features that I believe contribute to the typical increasing reluctance of students to compose as they advance through school. Very young children, or those with less experience in school music or formal music lessons, are much more responsive to the possibility of being able to compose than experienced or older students. Changing their perception of music from what somebody else creates to something anybody can create will produce open-minded learners and composers. That is the goal of pondering the question of "What is music?"

A fun way to start a music year, or music unit on composition then, is to begin by asking: What is music? What is music composition? What is the difference between music and noise? Can only humans make music?[1] Can noise be considered music? Draw students' awareness to the sounds (and noises) around them and how these are put together (and who put them together) and why we call some sounds *music* and others just *noise*. Listen to a wide variety of recordings to stimulate a discussion toward a class definition of music. Offer the following thought as a start for a useful discussion:

> Any sound can be a material used in music making. If a sound is conceived of as music, then it is music. Generally when a judge bangs his gavel it is not a musical gesture, but exactly the same gesture or sound could be part of music if it was conceived as such. The person who uses a sound as a musical statement is the only possible judge of whether it is musically valid or not. (Stevens, 2007, p. 2)

A Definition

After much discussion and listening to wide variety of musics, I share my favorite definition of music and music composition with students. This definition is broad, yet pinpoints the essence of music and composition, and makes sense to students of all ages:

> Music is organized patterns of sounds and silences, created by a human composer, to be expressive. Sounds can be high/low (pitch or melody), fast/slow (rhythm), loud/soft (dynamics), short/long (durations), and have different timbres. Composition is organizing musical sounds into logical, interesting, feelingful form.

With plenty of discussion, listening, and brainstorming activities, most students will come to these definitions, or close to them. Once students understand that music composition is simply the act of organizing sounds into a logical form, they begin to see themselves as capable composers.

Listen

As mentioned previously, it is critical to provide students with a wide and contrasting variety of music listening experiences. Music listening will undoubtedly and positively affect students' music understanding and composition abilities. As Bernstein pointed out, "All musicians write their music in terms of all of the music that preceded them" (1966, p. 271). Not only is an exposure to a wide variety of music beneficial, but using a variety of music to move beyond passive listening in the classroom is even better. Perceptive listening is the key to better musical understanding as well as more informed music composition skills. We need to help students listen in meaningful ways as they begin to explore their unique world of music composition.

In the book *What to Listen for in Music* (1985/1939), Aaron Copland provides a useful guide to describe different planes, or levels, of listening experiences. The first, and least complicated, approach to listening is on the *sensuous plane*. At this basic level, the most common for listeners, we listen to music simply for the pleasure of listening. In the second, *expressive plane*, listeners consciously relate to the music because of the feelings that it evokes. Copland wisely cautions that this does not mean there are specific and correct meanings or feelings associated with pieces of music. Rather, there are general feelings that each of us experience when listening to music expressively because of our personal life circumstances around music. Raising students' awareness of the kinds of feelings that are evoked for them when listening (and pointing out that each of us may have different feelings) helps to move them to this second plane. The third, and most sophisticated, plane of listening is what Copland terms the *sheerly musical plane*. Here one is drawn to the specifics of the composer's manipulation of the musical elements. It is at this level that one listens perceptively and musical understanding is enhanced. For student composers, listening at the level of the musical plane adds to their subconscious repertoire of tools for their own composing. As teachers, we want to move students to listen at that musical level.

The following listening lesson provides an activity that can lead to refined definitions of music as well as raise awareness of the wide variety of possible music. The recordings selected for this lesson are intentionally very different in order to illustrate the point of the lesson. Virtually any music can be used as long as it presents a drastically wide and varied range of styles, including music that is very contemporary (e.g., atonal, arrhythmic, or computer generated).

Lesson: What Is Music? What Is Music Composition?

Materials: Paper and pencils and the following musical recordings:

- "Idle Chatter" (track 1) from Paul Lansky's CD *More than Idle Chatter*. The recordings on this CD are computer generated from human voices. Upon first listening to "Idle Chatter," it is very difficult to ascertain what (or who) is actually creating the music.
- Any Beethoven or other classical symphonic music (I often use Beethoven's 5th Symphony because it is instantly recognized by most students).
- "Ridiculous" from the soundtrack to *Leaving Las Vegas*. This is the solo voice of actor Nicholas Cage singing a silly verse. It begins with background sounds as the movie set prepares for a take, the bell rings, somebody yells "Rolling," and then Cage begins to sing. At what point do we have "music"?
- "Money" on the Pink Floyd album *Dark Side of the Moon*. This track begins with the sound of a cash register, which highlights the use of nonmusical instruments in a music composition.
- "Thung Kwian Sunrise" is the first track on the CD *Thai Elephant Orchestra*, which indeed is performed by elephants. This track sounds very much like peaceful Asian gamelan music and stimulates, of course, some wonderful discourse about what it means to compose.

Procedure

1. Prepare students by telling them you will be playing five musical excerpts with the ultimate goal for them to determine the commonalities among all of them in order to come up with a definition of music and a definition of music composition. Ask them to listen to each excerpt and to write notes about what they hear (mostly to remember for discussion after hearing all of the excerpts).
2. Play each of the selections for approximately 1–2 minutes.
3. Organize students into small groups to discuss the music they heard, and ultimately come up with a definition of music and music composition that would encompass all of the selections.
4. Share the definitions from the groups, and discuss the definitions.
5. Reveal the titles and performers of the musical selections to lead to more discussion about what is means to compose music and what a music composition is (these prompts do not have right answers necessarily, but open up rich avenues for discussion).
6. Come together with an agreed upon class definition of *music* and *music composition* to set the foundation for continued exploration as composition.

Sensitivity to Sounds

Composer Pauline Oliveros has dedicated a lifetime of work and energy toward the study of what she labels *deep listening*. She has created several musical exercises (and compositions) that revolve around careful, thoughtful, quiet, deep listening. Deep listening "cultivates appreciation of sounds on a heightened level, expanding the potential for connection and interaction with one's environment, technology and performance with others in music and related arts" (downloaded from http://www.deeplistening.org/site/about, March 23, 2010). In the current noise-polluted and overstimulated environment that surrounds us all, it is useful (and refreshing) to take time to simply stop and listen. Careful, dedicated, deep listening (that is, sitting in silence for long stretches of time) will not only enhance our students' sensitivity to the sounds around them, but bring them to the third level of listening described by Copland—the sheerly musical plane—in a much more meaningful way.

Oliveros's book *Deep Listening: A Composer's Sound Practice* (2005) provides thoughtful exercises for musicians to improve their listening awareness. *Sonic Meditations* (Oliveros, 1974) contains twenty-five "prose compositions" that aid performers in listening more carefully and deeply to sounds around them. Children and adults of all skill levels and ages can use these and the other exercises to develop their listening awareness.

Listening maps provide another useful exercise for heightening students' listening abilities. Work by Kerchner (2000), Dunn (1997), and Blair (2007) provides interesting exercises for teachers to enhance students' musical understanding and perception of music by creating maps as they listen to music.

Listening Journals

A crucial piece of the listening puzzle is to have students keep a listening journal to raise students' awareness of all of the sounds and music that surround them on a daily basis and to make them conscious of the ways in which they listen to these.[2] Ask students to be conscious of sounds in their environment, ranging from ambient noises to the favorite music they listen to on their music devices, and to keep track of these sound experiences in listening journals. Ask them to think and write about how these sounds could be incorporated into a musical composition. An extension of a listening journal activity is to have students take turns with a small handheld recorder (or use their own cell phones) to capture a collection of daily sounds in their home environments and to share these with classmates. This activity could be finished by having students actually compose by organizing recorded sounds in a digital music software program such as Audacity (lesson 3D describes this composition lesson).

All of the listening activities should include discussion about what makes some of the sounds *music*, some *noise*, and how any of them might be used in a music composition. Heightened listening should continually contribute to students' repertoire and palette of musical possibilities as they develop into composers.

Aural Imagination

Although the previous discussions are about the external listening experience and developing sensitivity to all sounds, another kind of listening experience is the inner listening, or aural imagination. In the 1960s and 1970s, composer R. Murray Schafer created several wonderful "ear cleaning" exercises that were designed to stimulate the hearing imagination. *The Thinking Ear* (Schafer, 1986) provides a wealth of music listening and creating activities for teachers. *A Sound Education* (Schafer, 1992) provides "100 exercises in listening and sound-making" (p. 3). Both Schafer and Oliveros provide rich resources for teachers who want to expand the listening perception and listening imagination of their music students—a first and important step toward imaginative music composition.

I raise students' awareness of the power of their aural imagination through a technique called SCAMPER, which was first conceived by Alex Osborne. Bob Eberle (1996) created several SCAMPER games and activities to help improve children's imaginative ability in a book titled *Scamper: Games for Imagination Development*. The acronym SCAMPER is illustrated in figure 3.1.

Before doing a musical SCAMPER activity, introduce students to the concept of seeing, smelling, and hearing with their imaginations. To do this, ask students to close their eyes and try to imagine a place they've recently visited with family or friends. Then request that they "nod" when they can imagine this place using their imaginations. "Can you see the colors around you?" "Can you smell the smells"? (If not, ask them to visualize a zoo and imagine the smells of the elephant barn!) Finally ask, "Can you hear the sounds in this place? Are they loud? Soft?" and so forth. Unanimous nodding will ensure that students understand how to "image" with all of their senses. Next, take them through an extended visualization activity such as the following example taken from the Eberle book (1996) called "Sticks." It begins as follows:

- Take a stick about as long as your arm . . .
- Make it an old, weatherworn stick with the bark off . . .
- Make it crooked with knots in it . . .
- Make it rough . . .
- Make it gray . . .
- Do you have it?
- All right. Hold it out at arm's length and pretend that it's a snake . . . (Eberle, 1996, p. 22)

S ...ubstitute
C ...ombine
A ...dapt
M ...odify
    ...agnify
    ...inify
P ...ut to other
    uses
E ...liminate
R ...everse
    ...earrange

FIGURE 3.1 **SCAMPER**

And so on; the activity continues working the visual imagination until the stick ends up as a spotlight rotating with colored jewels on it. Create a variation on this idea by developing a SCAMPER exercise with music. Ask students to close their eyes and to imagine hearing the song "Twinkle Twinkle Little Star" (or any song that would be familiar to them). Again, after receiving a nod that the can imagine it, have them imagine this tune played very slow and very soft and very low by a tuba. Try to hear it played by a high, fast, and loud trumpet. How about a marching band playing "Twinkle Twinkle" as it marches down the street? Or a noisy rock band? And so on. Now the fun part. Ask the students to go back to hearing "Twinkle Twinkle" with just a piano playing. Now try to hear it backward. Upside down? Whether or not our students are able to literally hear a backward version of "Twinkle Twinkle" is not as important as them just messing around with musical sounds in their imaginations.[3] End these exercises by explaining that the ability to imagine sounds in different ways is an important skill of music composers who must think about the sounds they want to use in their music compositions.

Another aural imagination exercise I often do with students is to ask them to think about and conjure up the sounds they were hearing 24 hours previously (or 2 hours or 2 days). They sit quietly and slowly bring into their aural imagination the sounds from a place that they were previously. Next I may ask them to share one or two of their favorite sounds—either by creating them vocally or with body sounds, or on a given instrument. Extensions of this include improvising as a class with the sounds they imagined or breaking into groups and composing a composition with group members' imagined sounds realized with their voice or on instruments. The ability to imagine and manipulate sounds in one's aural imagination is important for musical growth and skill in music composition.

Explore

Because sound is the essence of one's musical composition palette, students should spend time listening to and exploring all the possibilities of sounds, be it from a solitary instrument, the sounds on the playground, or from the vast possibilities within the electronics of a MIDI synthesizer. As they explore sounds, they develop more perceptive listening skills, and with developed listening skills, sound exploration becomes more meaningful. The rich exploration of sounds should be a process that never ends. The most successful composers spend considerable time exploring the sound possibilities available in their palettes before making compositional decisions.

Explore all of the sound sources in the classroom that are not instruments. How can they be made into music? How can they make sounds that are different? Explore the infinite variety of sound possibilities from classroom instruments. Listen to the ways we can change the marimba sound by using different parts of the mallet or striking different parts of the instrument. As students explore, facilitate learning by using descriptors such as *high* and *low*, *fast* and *slow*, *loud* and *soft*, and *timbre* for different sounds. Eventually students should build a musical vocabulary of the words we use to describe sounds.

Gladys Moorhead and Donald Pond (1978/1951) completed a remarkable experiment in the 1940s in which they observed children as they played with musical instruments, sang musical songs, and made up musical games. Their study is noteworthy because it utilized qualitative methodology (unusual for that time period) using nonparticipant and in-depth observation of children engaged in music exploration over a long period of time (the first and only study of this magnitude). At any one time, 12 to 27 children, ages 1½ to 8½, spent time in the Pillsbury Foundation School in California surrounded by a rich array of percussive and melodic Asian instruments. For the most part, the program was very free, with the only formal organization occurring at lunch and rest periods. Although some of the older children had intermittent reading and writing lessons (presented in an informal manner), basically all of the children were left to explore the instruments and listen to any of a wide variety of available music recordings while at this school. The researchers observed, recorded, and ultimately analyzed the free musical play of the children over a 5-year period.

The researchers found that even without adult intervention, students spontaneously created music when given the opportunity to play around with the sounds that surrounded them. The importance of free experimentation and musical play in children's musical growth was a key finding of the study, and has been substantiated in other studies since (Berger & Cooper, 2003; Flohr, 2005; Levi, 1991; Littleton, 1991; Marsh & Young, 2006; Smithrim, 1997). "To produce his own music a young child's first need, we find, is freedom—freedom to move about in pursuit of his own interests and purposes, and free to make the sounds appropriate to them" (Moorhead & Pond, 1978/1951, p. 33).

As students explore the musical and found sounds of the classroom, they will discover that there is indeed an infinite possibility of sounds available for music composing. One caution is that exercises in listening and creative exploring of sounds should *not* be approached as having any correct "answer." Rules for steady beat and tonality should not enter the conversation or lessons at this point, unless they can be used to further more creative experiences. The point is to open students' music and sound worlds to the vast possibilities of music composition.

Setting up a Lesson

The remainder of this chapter provides six activities for listening, defining, and/or exploring music through music composition. As stated in chapter 1, these activities provide a springboard for additional music composition ideas from music teachers. You will notice in the procedures of several of the exercises that I often include directions to "give students the following steps to help guide their work" and then I provide a list. Ideally this list should be a written check-off form for the students to follow as they work. This is very helpful to keep them on track, and the elements of the list can then be used in an assessment rubric. Figure 3.2 provides an example of the type of worksheet that might accompany a lesson (it corresponds with lesson 3A).

Check off each item as you complete it:

_____ Find two sounds in the classroom that fit into each category below. Write the names of these sounds on the spaces below each of the categories:

high/low   **loud/soft**   **fast/slow**   **short/long**

_____   _____   _____   _____

_____   _____   _____   _____

_____ Choose one sound from each category. Circle your choices.

_____ Now create a short composition (at least 15 seconds) that uses the sounds you circled.

_____ Notate your composition on the paper provided using a different color to designate each sound.

FIGURE 3.2 Organizing Found Sounds

Composition Exercises

ACTIVITY 3A: Beginner: Found Sound Compositions

Rationale:
No matter where we are, our aural surroundings present a vast array of sound possibilities—with and/or without our manipulation. These sounds provide a rich palette to consider using and organizing into music compositions. The purpose of this lesson is to build an appreciation for, and sensitivity toward, the many sounds around us, and the potential for these sounds as elements in musical compositions.

Level/Type:
Beginning composers ages 9 and older. Groups of two or three students.

Materials:
- Any objects in the classroom
- Miscellaneous small objects from home (kitchen items, tools, coasters, etc.) placed around the room
- Large (at least 14 × 9) paper for their musical score
- Colored markers or crayons

Objectives:
Students will:
- Classify found sounds as high or low, soft or loud, short or long
- Organize found sounds into a composition
- Notate their found sound composition using graphic notation
- Perform their found sound compositions

Length:
Two to five class periods

Preparation:
Either review or introduce students to high/low, loud/soft, fast/slow, and short/long. Demonstrate by having the class sing in these different categories, and by showing how sounds around us fall into these categories. For example: *Listen to the birds outside. Are these high or low sounds? What about the sounds of the lights over head? Are they loud or soft? When I strike this bell, does the sound last or is it very short? What about when I tap a pencil on the desk? How can I make it sound lower?*
Make sure the classroom has plenty of safe noise-making objects around the room. Perhaps plant objects from home as potential music makers.

Procedures: Introduction. Ask students to select any small object from their backpack or desk or pocket. *Tap it or jingle it or shake it. Does it make a high or low sound? Is it loud or soft? Is the duration long or short?* Continue to explain how all sounds around us can be categorized as high/low, loud/soft, short/long, and can be "played" either fast or slow.

Step 1. Listen and categorize. With partners or trios, students should act as detectives and move about the room to experiment with and find different sounds. (Set the rules for items in the room that should not be touched; warn of not defacing or breaking any materials; musical objects that can be used must be played in a nontraditional manner.) One student of the pair or trio should be the scribe and write down the found sounds and categorize these as either high or low and loud or soft (premade sheets with these categories printed out can aid young children in this task). As students investigate found sounds, ask them to think about the following: *How can you change the sound from low to high and back? If it is a short duration, how might you make it longer (and vice versa)?*

Step 2. Let each group decide upon their two favorite sounds from each category (high/low, loud/soft, short/long) and circle or underline it on their paper (see figure 3.2 as a way to organize these sounds). Taking turns, have students from the groups either go to or pick up their favorite found sounds. If a group takes one that another group had selected as a favorite, they should make a second choice.

Step 3. *Using any combination of your favorite found sounds, compose a short composition. You can play your sounds in any way you want. It should last for at least 15 seconds. So that you can remember your composition, notate it on paper. Use a different color for each sound. Practice it several times so that you can perform it for class.*

Step 4. Perform the compositions. Discuss as appropriate and time allows (have performers explain their sounds, ask audience members to critique, etc.). Listen to the recordings of "real" compositions that utilize found sounds (see resource list below for music ideas).

Assessment: Are students able to:

✓ Categorize sounds as high/low? Loud/soft? Short/long?
✓ Notate and perform an original composition using their found sounds?

Extensions and
Variations:

- Students can make "found sound" instruments using materials from home to produce sounds for their compositions. (Harry Partch recordings would supplement this activity since he made several of his instruments!)
- Introduce timbre by having students group their found sounds into like-timbre groups. This might work well as an introduction to brass, woodwind, and percussion timbres.
- Stimulate a composition of found sounds with an abstract piece of art. Use the example of Earle Brown's *December 1952*, which is one of the first pieces written in graphic notation and for unspecified instruments. Two different recordings of this can be heard on his *Selected Early Works* CD to show how a score can be interpreted in different ways. The use of graphics creates rich possibilities for integrating lessons with the art teacher.
- Watch the video *STOMP-Live* (also available on YouTube) or listen to recordings where musicians use a variety of "found sounds" as their instruments (*Audio* by Blue Man Group or *Sugar Factory* with Evelyn Glennie and Fred Frith are two good examples).
- *Touch the Sound* DVD provides a wonderful exploration into the sound world of Evelyn Glennie, an award-winning percussionist who also happens to be deaf. Use this DVD as a launching point for discussion about sound exploration for music composition purposes.

Recordings and
Other
Resources:

- Blue Man Group. (1999). *Audio* [Audio CD]. New York: EMD/Virgin.
- Brown, E. (2006). *Selected Early Works* [Audio CD]. New York: New World Records.
- Creswell, L., & McNicholas, S. (Producers). (2008). *STOMP Live* [DVD]. USA: Well Go USA.
- Frith, F., & Glennie, E. (2007). *The Sugar Factory* [Audio CD]. New York: Tzadik.
- Partch, H. (1974). *Genesis of a Music: An Account of a Creative Work, Its Roots and Its Fulfillments* (2nd ed.). New York: Da Capo Press. This book contains wonderful color and monochrome pictures of Partch's invented instruments.
- Riedelsheimer, T. (Director). (2006). *Touch the Sound: A Sound Journey with Evelyn Glennie* [DVD]. USA: Docurama.

ACTIVITY 3B: Intermediate: Sound Spaces

Rationale: How often do we listen to the spaces around us and imagine they are part of a music-scape? As I sit in the relative quiet of my home, I become aware of the kitchen clock ticking, and then the heat coming on suddenly through the vents, covering the sound. The heat shuts off, and suddenly the ticking comes through. My sensitivity to these sounds and my aural imagination organized them into a musical piece. Raising awareness of the sounds around us as possible material for music heightens aural sensitivity and imagination. In the following composition activity, students are asked to draw upon sounds from spaces in different places and then replicate these sounds to re-create the space in a musical manner.

Level/Type: Beginner/intermediate. Group or individual.

Materials: • A variety of mallet and percussion classroom instruments

Objectives: Students will:
   • Recall ambient sounds from a previously shared space
   • Replicate ambient sounds on classroom instruments
   • Create a musical composition that replicates a space

Length: One or two class periods

Preparation: Lead students through a discussion and then an exercise in imagining, such as the exercise for imagining smells and sights in different places as described earlier in this chapter. Make sure students understand what it means to imagine if they are not already familiar with this term. Play one or all of Benjamin Britten's *Four Sea Interludes* ("Dawn," "Moonlight," "Sunday Morning," and "Storm") to illustrate how a composer used the corresponding spaces to compose for a symphony orchestra.

Procedures: Step 1. Ask students to name some of the spaces they have been in most recently. List on the board the spaces they discuss. These might be places such as the playground, a bus stop, their bedroom at night, the cafeteria, and so on. Narrow the list down to about four or five spaces that the majority of the students have experienced. Then ask them to imagine what the sounds are in those spaces.
   Step 2. Instructions: *Close your eyes and imagine all of the sounds you hear when you are in the school cafeteria.* Give them time to imagine many sounds. Have them list these. Ask for volunteers to share some of their sounds.

Step 3. Break students into groups. Each group should have a limited variety of classroom instruments such as one mallet instrument and a few varied percussion instruments. Assign each group one of the spaces they brainstormed from the first step. In their group they are to first figure out how to replicate sounds from this space on the traditional instruments, and then second to organize a musical composition that depicts this space and these sounds.

Step 4. Students perform the compositions for each other.

Assessment: Are students able to:
- ✓ Recall sounds from another space?
- ✓ Replicate these sounds on traditional classroom instruments?
- ✓ Organize their sounds into a musical composition that depicts a space?

Extensions and Variations:
- Assign spaces to groups without other groups knowing—students must guess the space after hearing their peers' compositions.
- Do this exercise with voices or traditional band or orchestra instruments.
- Use technology to capture sounds and then manipulate to simulate a space.
- Assign the same space (real or imagined) to all students, and see how different groups compose differently for the space.

Recordings and Other Resources:
- Britten, B. (1945). Four sea interludes from *Peter Grimes*. [Recorded by the Boston Symphony Orchestra]. On *Bernstein: The Final Concert* [Audio CD]. Berlin, Germany: Deutsche Grammaphon. (1992).
- Any other of the many recordings in which a composer uses a space as his or her inspiration.

ACTIVITY 3C: Advanced: Prose Composition

Rationale: Many of composer Pauline Oliveros's scores contain written instructions to the performers rather than traditional notation. This style has been described as "prose composition." The concept of writing instructions for players rather than writing musical notation is one that will open up students' understanding of musical as well as compositional possibilities.

This particular lesson is inspired by a piece by Oliveros titled "Mirror-rim," which she wrote, along with several other composers, when commissioned by saxophonist John Sampen and pianist Marilyn Shrude to contribute "postcard pieces" highlighting their unique musical style. The resulting CD, *Visions of Metaphor* contains a nice variety of composed, aleatoric and contemporary music. Oliveros' "Mirrorrim" is described as follows: "In a playful spirit appropriate to "The Postcards," Oliveros sent her score for Mirrorrim on a single postcard. The composition begins and ends on a concert E♭; otherwise, the score is entirely verbal. Improvisational instructions include: "If he goes up she goes down. If he goes down she goes up. Try to do this more or less simultaneously without knowing what the other is going to do. . . . PLAY. If you get confused it's part of the piece." (downloaded March 23, 2010 from: http://www.dramonline .org/albums/visions-in-metaphor/notes).

Level/Type: Intermediate/advanced. Individual.

Materials: • Recording of "Mirrorrim" by Pauline Oliveros
                  • Writing materials
                  • Instruments of any sort

Objectives: Students will:
                  • Write instructions for a music composition to be played by two others
                  • Perform a composition with written instructions

Length: One to two class periods for discussion and performances. Students should have a week or so to actually compose their "prose compositions."

Preparation: Examine several of Pauline Oliveros's musical compositions that are prose (these can be purchased from the Deep Listening website catalog). Provide students with the background information about Sampen and Shrude's commission to composers as well as Oliveros' subsequent "Mirrorrim" (described in the "Rationale" section above). John Cage's instructions for 4'33" would also provoke good discussion in preparation for this lesson.

Procedures: Introduction.

Step 1. Listen to "Mirrorrim" as a class, with the instructions given. Discuss how well the performers followed the instruction and how, given Oliveros' instructions, the piece could sound different. What are the minimum instructions one could give to ensure a performance that will follow a composers' intent?

Step 2. Each student is assigned (or chooses) two members of the class for whom they are to write a short (less than 5 minute) prose composition. Before leaving class, they should be aware of the instruments they will write for (it can be traditional instruments, voice, or classroom instruments).

Step 3. Remind students to think about the sounds they would like to hear and then imagine the best ways to write these in instructions. Pitch, duration, density, and other factors come into play.

Step 4. After one week (or more) working on the compositions, students share them with the class and their duos. The duos perform and feedback is given.

Assessment: Are students able to:

✓ Write composition instructions clearly enough for a duo of performers to interpret and perform?

Extensions and   • Rather than write for duos, students might write instructions for the
Variations: entire class as an ensemble.

• Pair with the language arts teacher to discuss using language as musical composition instructions. In Harry Partch's *Enclosure-Two*, there is an example where he combines unusual instrumental techniques and sounds with short texts.

• Compose music using diagrams or graphic notation such as music shown in the *Notations 21* sourcebook (Sauer, 2009) or on the liner notes to the Anthony Braxton CD *Creative Music for Orchestra*.

Recordings and   • Adams, J., et al. (1999). *Visions in Metaphor* [Recorded by John
Other   Sampen and Marilyn Shrude] [Audio CD]. Albany, NY: Albany Records.
Resources: • Braxton, A. (1990). *Creative Orchestra Music 1976* [Audio CD]. New
                      York: RCA Music.

• Partch, H. (2000). *Enclosure-Two* [Audio CD]. Saint Paul, MN: INNOVA Recordings.

• Lely, J., & Saunders, J. (2012). *Word events: perspectives on verbal notation*. London, England: Continuum. This book contains over 170 word scores from over 50 composers and provides excellent examples of word notation for students.

ACTIVITY 3D: Technology: Favorite Sounds

Rationale: The purpose of this project is for students to begin to explore, collect
                 and refine, and organize (and perhaps even invent) their favorite
                 sounds from the world around them as well as the rich world of
                 technology. As they add to and grow these digital "sound palettes"
                 they will have access to their own favorite types of sounds from
                 which to compose.

Level/Type: Intermediate.

Materials: • A recording device
                 • Computer stations with audio editing software such as *Audacity* or
                   Garage Band

Objectives: Students will:
                 • Collect sounds and organize them in a digital sound portfolio

Length: No determined time

Preparation: Organize computer stations with folders that are unique to each
                 student. Within these folders they will begin to collect and organize
                 a digital sound collection.

Procedures: Introduction. Ask students to collect a wide variety of digital sounds.
                 Explain that these can come from any space that they can record *or*
                 can be favorite digital sounds that they discover in MIDI instruments
                 or that they manipulate using audio editing programs. Each sound
                 should only be a "sample"—lasting no longer than 4 seconds.
                 Step 1. Students organize sound folders according to the sounds they
                 begin to collect and place their collected sounds into these folders.
                 Step 2. Students eventually use this bank of sounds as "color" for their
                 personal compositions.

Assessment: Are students able to:
                 ✓ Collect and organize a variety of digital sounds?

Extensions and   • Have students write about their favorite sound choices.
  Variations: • Students compose a sound collage that combines some of their
                   favorite digital samples.

ACTIVITY 3E: Ensemble: Just Scribble!

Rationale: Often we get stuck trying to select the first note in a composition. John Stevens, in his book *Search and Reflect* (2007) offers the idea of "scribbling" on an instrument in order to free up creative ideas. This activity begins with free improvisation as a way to generate ideas for something "composed" (able to replicate). In this exercise, taken from the Stevens text, students are encouraged to turn their scribbles into a composition. All students understand the concept of scribbling on paper; why not ask them to scribble on their instruments? (When introducing this idea to a workshop of teachers, one teacher lit up, "that's what my students do everyday before we begin our rehearsal!") And as Stevens himself offers, "Scribbling can be a liberating activity, freeing the mind from old habits and allowing musicians to interact spontaneously, without resorting to well worn clichés" (2007, p. 90).

Level/Type: Any.

Materials: Instruments (or voices)

Objectives: Students will:
- "Scribble" (improvise) freely on their instruments
- Compose a phrase based on a "scribbled" (improvised) pattern

Length: 15 minutes (warm-up)

Preparation: Make students conscious of their "scribbling" on their instruments before a rehearsal. Ask them to listen carefully to their own and another's scribble. Challenge them to scribble when practicing to see what kinds of musical ideas flow from their free play.

Procedures: Step 1. Write the words "SCRIBBLE" on the board as your warm-up activity. Give students approximately 5 minutes to play (or sing) freely on their instruments. They should focus on NOT editing their playing, but letting musical ideas flow quickly and freely.

Step 2. Stop and ask students to scribble once more, but to begin to listen to themselves and listen for a musical idea the length of a short phrase that they like. Give them 1 minute to find the phrase. (For older children, specific a two-measure length; shorter length for younger children).

Step 3. Once they find a phrase, they should repeat it several times in order to remember it.

Step 4. Go around the room and listen to student's original phrases.

Assessment: Are students able to:

    ✓ Find a phrase within their "scribble" and repeat it?

Extensions and   • Students write their phrases on manuscript paper and keep a
   Variations: portfolio of their weekly "Scribble phrases" (these could be in
       standard notation, or iconic or graphic notation).

    • The entire ensemble plays "call and response" with each member
      playing their phrase and the rest of the ensemble copying. Add
      Steven's extension of extending the phrase into a longer
      composition.

ACTIVITY 3F: A Listening Journal

Rationale: The listening journal provides an aid for teachers to better understand student listening habits and preferences, and for students to keep track of their growing awareness of, and sensitivity to music around them. This project can be configured in many different ways, depending upon the experience and age level of the student.

Level/Type: Appropriate for any level and age of students who are able to write. Individual work.

Materials: Notebook

Length: One week to one year or more. Listening journals could also be passed on from one music class to the next as students change teachers.

Preparation: If students are not used to keeping journals, then they would need some preliminary instruction about keeping a journal. A template page might be given to help guide them.

Procedures: Figure 3.3 offers an example of how a weekly listening journal might be organized. There are infinite ways this can be done, depending upon a teacher's purpose. As students keep track of music they hear, ask them to choose their favorite and least favorite from a week's worth of listening. Have them describe the musical elements of the pieces, and the musical and personal reasons for liking or disliking the music.

Instructions: *Use this journal to keep a list of all of the music you hear during the day. Each day write the titles (or description if you do not know the title) of music you hear during the day, and the place you are when you hear it. Choose one piece that is your favorite and one that is your least favorite from the week to describe in more detail. Use the format below for your descriptions:*

Favorite (least favorite) music title:

Composer/artist:

Describe the musical elements:

What musical elements make this piece your favorite (least favorite)?

What personal elements make this piece your favorite (least favorite)?

Share these through class discussions.

Assessment: The longer students keep listening journals, the more musically sophisticated their language should become as they describe the music they listen to. Students should grow in their musical sensitivity when listening and also extend their breadth of music listening experiences. There is no "right" or "wrong" to a listening journal and teachers should be careful not to assess the quality of these. Rather, listening journals should be used for class discussion or even for self-assessment. Assess whether the variety and depth of listening experiences changed over time. Ask students to keep track of this growth in their journals.

Extensions and Variations:
Use Copland's three listening planes (sensuous, expressive, musical) as rubrics for students to use to describe their listening experiences throughout the day (or in class).

Develop more categories for students to fill in their journals. For instance what music do they listen to in order to get going in the morning? (Their "wake-up and go" song). What is music they listen to when trying to sleep? (Their "fall asleep song"). What about when doing their homework? And so on. These categories might also become class playlists to accompany activities during the day.

Recordings and Other Resources:
• Riedelsheimer, T. (Director). (2006). *Touch the Sound: A Sound Journey with Evelyn Glennie* [DVD]. USA: Docurama.

Weekly Listening Log: Choose one 5-minute segment every day to write about your listening experiences.			
Day	**Place:**	**Music Heard:**	**Description (describe the sounds in detail):**
Mon			
Tue			
Wed			
Thur			
Fri			
Sat			
Sun			

FIGURE 3.3 Listening Journal Template

Compositional Prompts

Inspiration and Identity

Imagination is the outreaching of mind.
ROLLO MAY, *The Courage to Create*

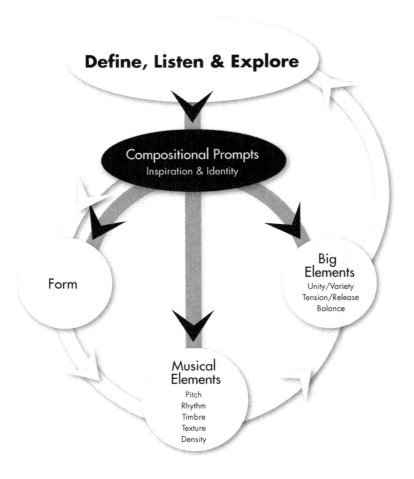

Shortly after giving a presentation to a group of music teachers about teaching music composition to children, I was asked a question that caught me off guard: "What materials do you use to inspire your students to compose?" This struck me in a curious way because, as silly as it sounds, I had not previously thought of the issue of inspiration as a motivator for composition. When working with students I would simply give them an assignment to compose, including the basic parameters for the assignment, and then go from there—after all, that's what we're supposed to do as teachers. For instance, I might have asked students to compose a melody in a new key we were learning, or compose a piece using X number of sounds on the synthesizer, or compose music that is in rondo form. All of these assignments are for the purpose of learning something technical about the craft of music—a valuable and legitimate approach to music composition. Many of the examples in this book fit into this category, which I would label "compose in order to learn about music." However, the question of how to *inspire* music composition, short of an assignment to compose, never really crossed my mind. But it now makes incredible sense, and I feel strongly that it is the key to successful and fulfilling music composition for students in our classrooms.

In music teaching (or *any* school subject, for that matter) teachers sometimes fall into the trap of giving assignments to meet objectives or standards without necessarily considering the potential for authentic inspiration for these assignments. Authentic music composition emerges from an inspiration—not *simply* from an assignment to compose (though it is likely that such an assignment may inspire further composition). More than the "academic" school subjects, music affords teachers the luxury to focus on inspiration and emotion, in addition to craft. This very simple realization has altered the way I teach music composition to students and hence to include this important step, not only early on in the process, but throughout all lessons. Although successful composition requires both imagination *and* craftsmanship, the quest for releasing our students' imaginations should come first. Imagination can easily be followed by the details of craft in music composition.

If not using students' own personal experiences as inspiration, I have found it effective to provide prompts, such as other art works, a story, a quote—anything *real* to work with—as inspiration for composing. This has led to great insight for me as a researcher/teacher and to the creation of some very profound compositions from students. It seems simple, this idea of providing something for inspiration, unless we get caught up in the technical side of composing, as I had, and ask students to follow only a technical prompt rather than an artistic prompt. Our students are bubbling over with potential inspiration grist for the artistic mill, and our job is to help them find and tap this rich source of imagination. I have had students compose music on a wide variety of topics ranging from girlfriends, lost fathers, favorite artists, to being kicked out of school. The music that comes from stories in their lives is the most powerful for them and often the most moving for the listener. Ideas for inspiration will be shared in this chapter before moving to the more "technical" aspects of composing as presented in later chapters. This is also how I suggest we approach teaching music composition with children in our classrooms.

Biographies and autobiographies of great artists seem to unanimously report that successful artistic processes require some technical craft, basic hard work, and inspiration. Just where the special muse comes from has been contested and debated. Inspiration may be internal, such as springing from a mood or a memory (e.g., Paul Lansky's *Memory Pages*), come from an external source such as a major historical event (e.g., John Adam's *On the Transmigration of Souls*, inspired by the events of 9/11), a painting (e.g., Morton Feldman's *Rothko's Chapel*, inspired by Mark Rothko's paintings), a poem (e.g., Beethoven's final movement of his *9th Symphony*, inspired by "Ode to Joy"), or even a hobby (e.g., Steve Reich's *Different Trains I. America: Before the War*, inspired by Reich's interest in train travel around the time of war). Word jazz artist Ken Nordine was inspired by, and composed music for, forty-four different colors (*Colors* CD)! Rich musical lessons can stem from the study of composers' inspiration and then lead to composition assignments that come from students' chosen inspirational events.

There are as many clues as there are artists who have talked about the mystery of inspiration. Some believe that you either have it or you don't, others feel that it is a gift from God, and yet others draw inspiration from very specific sources (Camphouse, 2002; Harvey, 1999). For some, it remains a mystery, as the author of *Music and Inspiration* points out:

> It is physical, comparable to the act of preparing to sing or play; it is spiritual, akin to a moment of religious revelation; it is sudden unpredictable, miraculous. It is all of these things, and yet it is a distinct, coherent experience. Musical inspiration, once experienced, cannot be confused with any other phenomenon. (Harvey, 1999, p. xiv)

Regardless of whether we verbally articulate what it is, we know that experiencing inspiration is an important part of being human. Inspiration for music, just as inspiration for living, is essential to the creative process and a fulfilling life.

Students enter our classrooms with a fire of creative inspiration waiting to be kindled and stoked in arts classes. Finding and fueling their inspirational muse is the focus of this chapter. How do we move students forward from simply composing music because it is an assignment to composing music from an authentic inspiration? In this chapter I present ideas on inspiration and prompts that might inspire in three sections: "Tapping the Muse," "Compositional Identity," and "What Is Your Commission?" I conclude the chapter with a section on ideas for how teachers might balance the impulse of inspiration with technique—that is, the balance of freedom and structure.

Tapping the Muse

We all hope that our students desire, and enjoy, learning about music. How might we also inspire them to compose their own music? The romanticized view of the most lionized nineteenth-century composers is that they experienced nothing short of psychological break-downs while writing their best music. Revolutions, winter melancholy, and lost love were the inspirations for composers such as Beethoven, Schubert, and Wagner. What "sturm and drang" could a 12-year-old possibly have that would create the need or desire to compose? Ask them. Although they may not be carrying the same emotional baggage of prodigy Frédéric Chopin, every child holds the potential for creative inspiration just waiting to be tapped. I learned this most poignantly in my work with high-needs adolescent men at a residential facility in Chicago.[1] Their stories and inspirations came from their everyday lives. Following is an example from one of my students to illustrate this potential.[2]

Real Inspiration

Myles, at 18 years old, was one of the oldest of my eight students. He would show up to our weekly class in the same manner: he would hurry in, politely say hello to me, and then move off to his "studio" (a small bathroom/closet attached to the classroom) and begin composing on a MIDI synthesizer using a music sequencing program and computer. He would sing and sing and sing into the microphone, and record over and over until the musical tracks he had created were to his satisfaction. His songs were about love and the happiness and sadness of times with a girlfriend, or missing his father (whom he had not seen lately because they didn't "see eye to eye"). The titles of his compositions reflect his passions in life: "Dad," "Weary," "Break-Up," "God," and "Salvation." He had many things to express through his music and explained to me he had been simply waiting for an opportunity to finally record his "songs."[3] When I asked Myles whether he composed before, he replied that he had composed many songs since he was at least 10 years old. He had carried around this "music" in a folder—which I discovered was pages and pages of lyrics written on scraps of paper. It's just that he never had the opportunity to record them. When I asked if he could remember the "tune" to any of the lyrics he had written when he was 10, he assured me that he could.

A powerful discovery that I learned when working with this particular group of young men was that their *muse* came from many sources. The rather dire circumstances of some of their lives naturally prompted inspiration for many of their compositions. However, the daily soundscapes of these students'—and all students'—lives are pervasive, and sometimes unconsciously influential, in their music compositions. I discovered, as Burnard (2000) found, that "fashioning pieces from known melodies and rhythms 'picked up' 'by ear' from popular music or instrumental repertoire was a common experience expressed by many of the children. Not surprisingly, they seemed to store-and-draw ideas from known and existing pieces" (p. 234). A counselor who had observed the particular group of young men that I had worked with at the group home offered a particularly poignant insight: "Their music and lyrics were in this sense, an honest tour of their minds."

The music our students hear while shopping at Target, playing video games, or on their ipods clearly influences their compositions. Beethoven's "Ode to Joy" melody was popular with one young man, whereas the Boyz II Men hit "It's So Hard to Say Goodbye" influenced another. Although all of our students are not in the same situations as the high-needs students I have worked with and continue to work with, I have found that for any child, of any age, finding the muse for inspiration takes little effort if given time and space. A wealth of music exists within all children—composing provides an opportunity for it to be expressed. Perhaps nothing is more important or inspiring than giving students this chance to tell *their* stories and share *their* experiences through music composition rather than spending so much time getting them to sound like composers of the past, or even to sound like us.

Relating to Other Arts

> Many of the questions about the relationship between the visual arts and music posed by earlier modernist artists . . . have stubbornly refused to disappear; on the contrary, they have continued to occupy the minds of a wide variety of painters, sculptors and musicians whose styles and tendencies, aesthetic convictions and political affiliations are otherwise bewilderingly different. (Vergo, 2010, p. 351)

Music's sister arts provide not only great inspiration for music composition, but also rich fodder for integrated arts lessons (see, for example, lesson 4F at the end of this chapter) or lessons with teachers of other subjects. It is well documented that many composers have been inspired by other art forms and vice versa. Two particular books provide rich examples of music inspired by art (Evans, 2003) and art inspired by music (Vergo, 2010). Sauer's *Notations 21* (2009) highlights hundreds of beautiful notations that could stand alone as works of visual art. These resources could provide wonderful inspiration for music composition or improvisation and collaborations with a visual arts teacher.

It is useful to learn about the prompts that inspire composers by reading liner notes or transcripts of interviews that describe their inspirational prompts. One source that I have found particularly helpful for learning about contemporary composers and their compositions is a website called DRAM (http://www.dramonline.org/). It is described as "a scholarly resource of recordings, including CD quality audio, liner notes and essays from New World, Composers Recordings, . . . and other important labels."

Gathering ideas about how other composers create and are inspired by other arts provides endless ideas for potential composition prompts for our students. Earle Brown, a contemporary of John Cage and active jazz musician and composer, was particularly interested in visual art and sculptors to inspire his music (Vergo, 2010). Brown's composition *December 1952* is credited as one of the first graphic scores to be published and presents a wonderful image for students to ponder as music notation. Though Brown does not specifically credit Mondrian, it is very similar in ideas to Mondrian's *Composition in Lines*. The score contains thirty short lines of different thickness arranged on a page. The performer can begin and end at any point and interpret the score in any way. Brown's own explanation is fascinating to read and provides an insight that would no doubt interest students:

December 1952 specifically is a single page, something like a photograph of a certain set of relationships of these various horizontal and vertical elements. In my notebooks at this time I have a sketch for a physical object, a three-dimensional box in which there would be motorized elements, horizontal and vertical, as the elements in December are on the paper. But the original conception was that it would be a box which would sit on top of the piano and these things would be motorized, in different gearings and different speeds and so forth so that the vertical and horizontal elements would actually physically be moving in front of the pianist. The pianist was to look wherever he chose and to see these elements as they approached each other, crossed in front of and behind each other, and obscured each other. I had a real idea that there would be a possibility of the performer playing very spontaneously, but still very closely connected to the physical movement of these objects in this three-dimensional motorized box. This again was somewhat an influence from Calder: some of Calder's earliest mobiles were motorized and I was quite influenced by that and hoped that I could construct a motorized box of elements that also would continually change their relationships for the sake of the performer and his various readings of this mechanical mobile. I never did realize this idea, not being able to get motors and not really being all that interested in constructing it. (Brown, 2008, p. 3)

Moods as Inspiration

How might one compose to sound angry? Happy? Depressed? Sad? Using these prompts about feelings that all students have is a wonderful way to connect feeling with, and teach about, concepts in music. Put students in small groups with any types of musical instruments, and give them an emotion (e.g., angry, sad, happy, sleepy, excited, bored) to compose music to. Simply ask them to compose music that both represents the emotion and is something that they can replicate (encourage them to write notes or draw some kind of graphic reminders so they can reproduce their music at a later time). A similar exercise is to provide students with some of the common *emoticons* they know from their text messaging world (see figure 4.1). Have them work in groups to come up with a short composition using any variety of instruments or voices that depicts their assigned emotion. The point here is to have them think about constructing sounds in such a way as to portray feelings— from their own perspectives. The groups might perform for one another while other students try to guess which feeling inspired the composers. Another variation is to ask students to compose a piece of music that represents their own moods at different times during a

FIGURE 4.1 Emoticons for Composition (downloaded from http://www.myemoticons.com/)

particular day. (What is their mood when waking up in the morning? Going to school? Being in school? Playing at recess? How would they compose music to highlight these moods?)

I avoid linking *sad* with minor or *happy* with major. It is more interesting to see what students create and talk about when describing their music. After individuals or groups of students have performed their "emotion" pieces for one another, open the discussion: Why is it that slow, soft, often arrhythmic and minor pieces suggest a sad aura? Or just the opposite for a more "happy" emotion? Does composing sad music make one sad? Does listening to sad music make one sad?

Listen and compare the traditional and emotionally charged "favorites" such as the endings to Tchaikovsky's *1812 Overture* or *Elsa's Procession to the Cathedral* by Richard Wagner. Or compare the original *Adagio for Strings* by Samuel Barber (often considered very emotional music) to DJ artist Tiësto's remix of this composition (very upbeat). How does a John Philip Sousa march compare to Morten Lauridsen's *O Magnum Mysterium*? What is it about mariachi and salsa music that makes one want to dance and feel happy? The point of these activities is to draw attention to the power of music to convey and stir human emotions—not that there is a right way to compose in order to do so. These discussions should move beyond (or in spite of) the technical craft, and focus on the gestalt of what makes music move us. These discussions should not lead to right or wrong answers, but rather stimulate thought and reflection that will inspire meaningful and emotionally charged music composition.

Cross-Curricular Fun

Just as other arts and moods can provide inspiration for composition, so can studying other subjects, such as through connecting themes from units to ideas for composition. Imagine if students, instead of writing a paper, were given the option to compose music based on a social studies class unit on slavery? Or perhaps they are given the chance to use their knowledge of poetic forms to compose music for voice. The potential of musical composition as an alternative route for demonstrating their understanding may be a motivating option for many students, and linking music composition to the other arts can provide ideal inspiration to do such.

Compositional Identity

"Just as Mozart sounds like Mozart, and Chopin sounds like Chopin, Beatrice sounds like Beatrice. Each piece is different, but nevertheless, there are features that make it possible to identify her writing" (Upitis, 1992, p. 96). Researchers have learned that children can develop unique musical styles, when given the chance, very early in their composition experiences (Burnard, 2000; Burnard & Younker, 2004; Hickey, 2009; Stauffer, 2002, 2003; Upitis, 1990, 1992; Younker, 2000, 2006). Each one of us and each of our students has a musical identity and style as unique as our fingerprints. After only a short time composing, and given the freedom to develop, the unique compositional identities of our students will begin to emerge.

By *compositional identity* I mean the unique personality and musical style that is revealed in a child's compositions. Identity is linked to inspiration in that it is real, it is emotional, it is personal, and it aids in the expressing of one's musical voice. It provides the means for composers to express their deepest, often ineffable, feelings. For some, this is cathartic. As described previously, the importance of inspiration and identity as prompts for composition has been reinforced through my experience working with adolescent and high-needs youth. These students tell their stories through their unique music compositional voices and it is up to the teacher to afford the time and space for their personal narratives to emerge. Sharing one's unique identity through music composition is a powerful outlet for creativity and imagination in music making.

An improvisation exercise that works to highlight one's musical identity (or present mood) is to gather around a circle of instruments and ask students to improvise their "personality" for that day (or their personality in life). A short riff is all that is needed and could even offer an effective start to every class period in order to gauge the dispositions for that day. An extension would have students develop these riffs into solo compositions that depict who they are as musician/creators. (See lesson 4A at the end of this chapter for a variation of this exercise.)

Over a period of time, a personal portfolio of compositions should be collected and reflected upon in which students begin to describe their unique compositional identity as it begins to emerge. As students collect and add to their portfolio of compositions (ideally over several years, if not at least an entire school year), have them write about themselves as composers, much like composers do when writing their own biographies. When they compile their first CD of their music, have them write their biographies in a way that describes their musical style. What is their favorite instrumentation to write for? Why? How would they describe their composition style? Who or what inspired their style? Use examples from composers' liner notes or their personal web pages (see the example by Earle Brown above). This development of composition identity is not only authentic, but it will provide motivation to continue to compose and develop as a composer.

> Once people become aware that music is in themselves and not only in those who have been selected to become musicians, once they take back to themselves the musical act in a spirit of delight and self-affirmation, who knows what else they might insist on reclaiming, and enjoying, of what has been taken from them? (Christopher Small, in Stevens, 2007, p. iv)

What Is Your Commission?

"I believe that a real composer writes music for no other reason that it pleases him. Those who compose because they want to please others, and have audiences in mind, are not real artists" (Schoenberg, 1984, p. 54). While Schoenberg may have had the ideal situation in mind, we all know that one authentic form of "inspiration" is a commission to compose for certain ensembles, and by extension, audiences. The inspiration in these cases is bound by the parameters of the ensemble that will perform the music, the length given for the performance, the deadline date, as well as the audience for whom it is intended. As students develop their skills and begin to venture into different sorts of repertoire for composition, discussion about "commission-type" parameters raises students' awareness about choices in shaping their music compositions.

Discuss with students what their compositions would sound like if written for the following audiences:

- A best friend
- A significant other
- Church
- A grandparent
- A funeral
- A baby
- A fancy award ceremony
- MTV
- A radio station
- A commercial

Depending on the audience, decisions about length, volume, tempo, instrumentation, lyrics, and so forth, need to be carefully made. Composing to "commissions" with an audience in mind (or trying to sell a product) provides students with inspiration for making musical and artistic choices. An authentic "commission" would be to assign a music composition project that would really be used, such as background music for morning school announcements, music for playing in the hallway as students move to classes, music for the lunchroom, and so on.

Balance of Freedom and Structure

How can we strike a balance between allowing students to simply find and follow their muse and providing rules for structure? This balance between freedom and structure, also discussed in chapter 2, is one of the biggest issues facing music teachers. When it come to inspiration, however, freedom *must* come before structure, which will motivate the desire to learn about structure in order to express more effectively. Composing in an authentic manner—one that is inspired by one's personal voice and inspiration—will invariably lead to students wanting to learn more technique toward achieving a desired musical end. Providing such freedom will drive the need to know more.

One's compositional identity should be reflected upon and honored and probed and developed from the very beginning of music composition activities. The point of music composition is not to sound like the teacher, but to sound like oneself. The journey to find and shape one's musical voice can last a lifetime. It should not be squelched in the classroom, but discovered and nurtured through every composition experience.

Music holds great potential to inspire and move all human beings. I maintain a folder of what I call "beautiful" music on my iPod. It includes a collection of music that creates goose bumps every time I listen. Selections include Lauridsen's *O Magnum Mysterium*; *Gabriel's Oboe*, by Ennio Morricone, from the movie *The Mission*; the amazing English horn solo in the Largo movement of Dvorak's *Symphony No. 9*; and *Danny Boy* (the band version as well as a vocal rendition by John McDermott). I also have a folder of music to listen to when I need a boost during a run or when I am at the gym. We can all point to such music, and perhaps as teachers we can help students identify their "goose-bumps" music. What do students list as their "beautiful" music? What are their "power" songs? What is on their iPods? Do you know? The answers can provide a window into understanding our students as human beings as well as composers. Early in the composition process, this discussion should take place with students: What inspires you? How can you organize sounds to capture and convey this very inspiration? These questions will lead to meaningful compositions and then curiosity for how to compose better.

What I have learned in my work with students and what has subsequently shaped the curricular structure that I am suggesting here, is that before we approach composition as an assignment with rules for length, number, and kinds of notes and rhythms, and other technical issues, we should begin by using inspiration as a way to open the door for students to compose. What does it take for a teacher to inspire? The inspiration for music composition in the classroom should be the easiest of teachers' tasks. Letting go and allowing students to connect to real-life events and music in their lives will fire inspiration for their music compositions and provoke students to not only learn more about music, but enjoy using music composition as a vehicle to express. Students do not need rules yet—they simply need tools and space and time to create. Although the following sample activities certainly do not solve the mystery of inspiration, it is my hope that they provide teachers with tools to allow the creative spirit to unfold.

Composition Exercises

ACTIVITY 4A: Beginner: Who Are You?

Rationale:	It is important to establish early on with students that their unique selves should also produce a unique compositional self. Students should compose to tell their stories and give voice to their identities rather than to sound like how the teacher hopes for them to sound. This can happen if freedom is given at the beginning of composition exercises and musical identity is brought to the forefront of the conversation and discussion.
Level/Type:	Beginning composers of any age. Individuals.
Materials:	• A wide variety of classroom instruments or voices or found sounds • Paper and writing tools
Objectives:	Students will: • Compose short musical compositions that reflect their personal identity
Length:	One or two class periods
Preparation:	Arrange a wide variety of classroom instruments around the room in "stations." Each station should contain at least one mallet, one percussive instrument, and one miscellaneous instrument. As students come into the classroom, instruct them to find a station of their choice. Give them time to move around and explore the different instruments and sound choices.
Procedures:	Step 1. After about 5 minutes of exploration on instruments, ask students: *Who are you today?* They may provide a variety of answers. Step 2. *Rather than tell me who you are, I would like you to compose a short piece of music using any of the instruments in your station that describes who you are today. You may use all or just one of the instruments at your station as well as your voice. Explore and create, and when you are finished, write down your composition on the paper provided in any way so that you can remember it.* Give them permission to move instruments around if it is important to their composition. (15 minutes) Step 3. Allow volunteers to share their compositions. Ask them to explain the choices they made. Step 4. Put the composition notations into individual folders for continued work on these "identity" compositions.

Assessment: Are students able to:

     ✓ Compose to the prompt "Who are you today?"

     ✓ Notate their composition?

     ✓ Perform and describe their composition?

Extensions and
 Variations:

- Repeat this exercise throughout the year (or over several years!). At the end of the year, ask students to pick their favorite or most telling compositions and write about themselves as a developing composer.
- Extend the exercise into a longer composition exercise in which students compose a "biography" of an important time in their lives. (This may link nicely to a writing class in which they are writing vignettes or short autobiographies.)
- Adapt this lesson for other types of classes such as guitar, keyboard, or computer.

ACTIVITY 4B: Intermediate: Inspired by an Event

Rationale: Many composers have written music that was inspired by an important
                 event in their lives or in history. Epic historical events are prime
                 inspiration for expression through music. Events might inspire literal
                 music representation or abstract, and examples of both lead to
                 deeper understanding of music as both a representative and abstract
                 art. Although our memories serve as powerful reminders of past
                 events, music allows composers to recall through a creative medium.
                 Children and adults alike can organize musical sound in ways that
                 are inspired by events, and this is often one of the most accessible
                 ways to start composing.

Level/Type: Intermediate. Individual or groups.

Materials: • Any variety of instruments or voice

Objectives: Students will:
                 • Compose music in groups to depict a familiar event
                 • Perform their original music

Length: Two (or more) class periods

Preparation: Select a variety of recordings that illustrate music composed based
                 on historical or personal events in composers' lives. The selections
                 listed in this lesson offer one possible sampling.

Procedures: Introduction. Play excerpts from the following recordings:
                 1. Charles Ives's "The Fourth of July," movement III, from the *Holiday
                    Symphony*, which is actually a suite of boyhood recollections of the
                    Fourth of July, Washington's Birthday, Decoration Day, and Thanks-
                    giving (any of these movements would be appropriate).
                 2. *On the Transmigration of Souls*, by John Adams (commissioned
                    by the New York Philharmonic to honor the victims of the 9/11
                    attacks). An interesting point to discuss is that Adams described
                    this piece as a "memory space."
                 3. *Come Out*, by Steve Reich. Reich takes a phrase recorded from a
                    young African American man who was assaulted and hoped to go
                    to jail for protection. The one phrase "come out to show them" is
                    looped until it is no longer recognizable.

                 After listening to these recordings, discuss how it is the composer used
                 the events to compose their music. How are they different? How did
                 they use moments from the event to inspire the music? Which are
                 more representative? Which more abstract? What devices did the
                 composers use to make the recordings interesting to the listener?

Step 1. Have students work in groups to select an event (recent or past, local or national) that is of interest to them. (Events could also be preselected by the teacher or taken from a recent lesson in social studies or history.)

Step 2. Students work together to compose a piece of music that illustrates, in either abstract or representative ways, the event they chose. They should title their music.

Step 3. Groups perform for the class.

Assessment:
Are students able to:
- ✓ Select an event that is appropriate and lends itself to an inspired musical composition?
- ✓ Compose music to their selected event?
- ✓ Perform the original music compositions?

Extensions and Variations:
- The entire class works on single event composition perhaps in conjunction with a social studies or history unit.
- Compose for a school event/celebration such as an anniversary of the school founding or African American History Month.
- Work with the art teacher to compose music inspired by different visual artists (see lesson 4F).

Recordings and Other Resources:
- Ives, C. (1913). *Keeping Score: Ives, Holidays Symphony* [Recorded by the San Francisco Symphony] [Audio CD]. San Francisco, CA: San Francisco Symphony Studio (2009).
- Adams, J. (2002). *On the Transmigration of Souls.* [Recorded by the New York Philharmonic] [Audio CD]. New York: Nonesuch Records (2004).
- Reich, S. (1966). Come Out. On *Steve Reich: Early Works* [Audio CD]. New York: Nonesuch Records (1992).

ACTIVITY 4C: Advanced: Memory Pages

Rationale: Paul Lansky's music "Memory Pages" is described as "a few personal memories my wife Hannah Mackay and I have had, along with thoughts about remembering and the passion of time" (from the CD liner notes). The music is an interesting combination of voice and computer-generated sounds. The voice tells a story of both Lansky's and Mackay's memories. It is an interesting combination of text and music woven together. This music will provide a model of how students can combine text through voice and instrument (computer or otherwise) to compose music that brings alive a personal memory.

Level/Type: Advanced. Pairs. (Could be done on computer.)

Materials:
- A variety of percussion instruments (or computer sequencing software)

Objectives: Students will:
- Create a poetic text that describes a vivid memory from their past
- Compose music that combines the text with percussion instruments (that either they themselves play or write for others to accompany them while they read their text).

Length: Two weeks: One class period for an introduction and text writing. One week for students to work. One or two class periods for performances.

Preparation: None.

Procedures: Step 1. Play "Memory Pages" (13:05) for the class. Discuss the music before sharing the background of the piece. Then provide the information about the music (see Rationale above).

Step 2. Students create a "memory" text that describes a memory from their childhood past. It should be in poetic style verse (as opposed to narrative or storytelling) and no longer than two 4-verse stanzas.

Step 3. Students work in pairs to read each others' texts and offer comments and suggestions.

Step 4. Students compose a musical piece for percussion instruments (solo or more) and their "memory" text. The text they write (step 2 above) can be repeated or broken into parts as need be. (The piece should be notated, but it can be graphic notation.)

Step 5. Students rehearse their "memory pages" (as solo percussion and voice or for other percussionists).

Step 6. Students perform their music.

Assessment: Are students able to:

✓ Create poetic text that describes a memory from their past?

✓ Compose music for percussion and voice using the text?

✓ Perform as soloists (or with others) their percussion and voice "memory pages" compositions?

Extensions and Variations:

- Compose the original memory text for voices only (such as a chorus).
- Use memory text to inspire an instrumental composition (no voice).
- Take prewritten text (such as a famous poem or speech from history) and combine with percussion instruments into a music composition.
- Combine spoken words with guitar in a guitar class.

Recordings and Other Resources:

- Lansky, P. (1994). Memory Pages. On *More Than Idle Chatter* [Audio CD]. Bridge Records.

ACTIVITY 4D: Technology: Soundscapes

Rationale:	Who decides where music begins and noise ends? What frames a musical composition, if not a notated score? Christopher DeLaurenti is a Seattle based composer and "phonographer" who raises these philosophical questions about music as he records places, unedited, as his musical works. DeLaurenti describes phonographers as "sound artists, composers, and recordists who improvise live in real-time with unprocessed field recordings collected around the world" (from http://www.delaurenti.net/music.htm). These spaces inspire his thinking as a composer and musician, and also inspire listeners to think about boundaries of music. In this lesson, students will go one step further by not only acting as phonographers in recording sounds from a favorite place, but they will then manipulate them into a musical composition.
Level/Type:	Intermediate/advanced.
Materials:	• Digital recording devices for each student (e.g., computer, cell phone, handheld recorder) • Computer stations with audio manipulation software (Audacity is a free, cross-platform software program that would work well for this assignment)
Objectives:	Students will: • Record at least 10 minutes of unedited sound from a place of their choice • Using the recording as a base, manipulate the audio file (cut, shorten, move around, sound effects, etc.) into a music composition • Provide a paragraph to describe the space they recorded as well as their intention for the final composition
Length:	Two to four classes
Preparation:	Students will need some knowledge of an audio editing program.
Procedures:	Introduction. (day 1) Listen to selections from Chris DeLaurenti's CD *Favorite Intermissions* and other recent recordings from his website. Discuss the concept of a "phonographer" and DeLaurenti's approach to music composition. Step 1. (outside of class) Students will record 10 minutes of a sound space of their choice. Encourage them to find a place that has either plenty of rich sounds or a variety of interesting sounds. In other words, think about the sonic space before recording it for the composition.

Step 2. (day 2) Students work on manipulating their audio file into a musical composition using an audio editing program. They write a paragraph describing their original space recording and the thoughts that went into shaping their final composition.

Step 3. Play student compositions for the class (or have students swap compositions and perform for one another). Ask the composer to describe how she organized her composition.

Assessment:	Are students able to: ✓ Compose a "soundscape" composition using a recording audio file? ✓ Describe the technology process and conceptual thoughts behind the musical soundscape?
Extensions and Variations:	• More extensive computer software understanding can provide more complicated procedures such as overdubbing, inserting, pitch bend techniques. • Exchange audio recorded spaces with classmates who would then manipulate these into a composition.
Recordings and Other Resources:	• DeLaurenti, C. (2009). Found Soundscape: C-SPAN Presidential Inauguration, January 20, 2009 [MP3]. Retrieved from http://www.and-oar.org/pop_andp34.html. • DeLaurenti, C. (2010). *Favorite Intermission: Music Before and Between Beethoven, Stravinsky, Holst* [Audio CD]. New York: GD Stereo. Any selection from this work will suffice. • http://www.delaurenti.net/

ACTIVITY 4E: Ensemble: Exploration Etude

Rationale: A composition teacher I know gives his students "etude" assignments in order to hone certain composition skills. That is, they are to compose relatively short exercises designed to focus on only one or two ideas. The dictionary definition of etude is "a composition featuring a point of technique but performed because of its artistic merit." The point of an etude exercise here is to bring a little more focus to the exploration of sounds into a music composition that is inspired by playing around and improvising on one's instrument (or voice). This also acquaints students with the musical concept of etude. (This etude exercise would work well in any of the components of the composition curriculum.)

Level/Type: Intermediate. Solo.

Materials: • Musical instrument
  • Manuscript paper

Objectives: Students will:
  • Create a short etude for their instrument (or voice)
  • Notate their composition using standard notation so that others are able to perform it

Length: One to three class periods

Preparation: Examples of short etudes for instruments include "The Elegy for Mippy II" and "The Waltz for Mippy III for tuba," both written by Leonard Bernstein in honor of his brother's beloved dog. These short pieces illustrate how a composer writes for the character of the instrument. There are etudes written for virtually every instrument and voice, and they present an accessible way for students to think about first composing for their instrument. This lesson might be introduced in a full ensemble class, with the assignment for students to work on the etude outside of class and then share after a period of time. If students regularly have lessons (in addition to full ensemble), then this lesson works best during a lesson period.

Procedures: Step 1. (This can be done in a full ensemble as a warm-up activity.) *Improvise around on your instrument until you find some interesting phrases you like. Play around, and then repeat what you like until you can remember it. This will become the basis for your etude.*
  Step 2. After improvising and then repeating and finding some interesting phrases, students will then compose and notate an original etude for their instrument. The etude should be at least 16 measures.

Step 3. Students notate their etudes and play them. (It is optional to perform for class or ask others to perform their notations.)

Assessment: Are students able to:

✓ Compose a short etude that they can play on their instrument?

✓ Notate their etude with enough detail for others to perform it?

Extensions and Variations:

- Write an etude for an instrument or voice different from your own
- Compose an etude dedicated to a favorite cartoon character (or pet, or sports hero, etc.).
- Create a multi-etude composition that includes three or four etudes that work well together (e.g., fast, slow, dance-like).

Recordings and Other Resources:

- Cage, J. (1934). Six Short Inventions for Seven Instruments [Recorded by Manhattan Percussion Ensemble, David Tudor, John Cage, and Maro Ajemian]. On *The 25-Year Retrospective Concert of the Music of John Cage* [Audio CD]. Mainz, Germany: WERGO (1994).
- Bernstein, L. (1948). Elegy for Mippy II for Solo Trombone and Waltz for Mippy III for Tuba [Recorded by the New York Philharmonic]. On *Joseph Alessi Plays Bernstein, Peaslee, Rush, Ewazen, et al.* [Audio CD]. BCCS Classics (2006).

(Performances of these two etudes and many others can also be found on YouTube.)

ACTIVITY 4F: Arts Together Inspire

Rationale: It is not at all unusual to find multiple artists in multiple fields finding inspiration from each other across the arts. Paintings, sculpture, and poetry provide wonderful grist for inspiration in composition. This lesson was inspired by one that my colleague Dr. Janet Barrett and I did with middle school students. It uses concepts on integrating the arts from Barrett, McCoy, and Veblen's (1997) text *Sound Ways of Knowing*.

Level/Type: Beginner through advanced. Groups or individual.

Materials:
- Selected paintings: "Twittering Machine," by Paul Klee, and any one from Morton Feldman, as well as a variety of other art (abstract art from artists such as Andy Warhol, Salvador Dali, Paul Klee, and Wassily Kandinsky seem to work best for this lesson)
- Selected recordings: ("California Counterpoint," by Cindy McTee, "Rothko Chapel," by Morton Feldman, and any of the tracks from "Ken Nordine's Colors," by Ken Nordine)
- *Colors* book by Ken Nordine
- GarageBand software, or any instruments if technology is not available
- Paper and writing tools (or equivalent on a computer)

Length: At least two class periods

Preparation: Prepare the classroom by hanging a variety of abstract paintings around the room, including the ones mentioned in this lesson. Discuss with students the kinds of inspirations that artists find from other artistic venues. Play and discuss the following musical selections, and show the visual art: "California Counterpoint," by Cindy McTee, inspired by Paul Klee's "Twittering Machine"; "Rothko Chapel," inspired by Mark Rothko's paintings, and Ken Nordine's "Colors," inspired by colors (Nordine created a book and CD of his work, *Colors*, which had its creative origin in a marketing campaign for the Fuller Paint Company).

Procedures: Step 1. Have students walk around the "gallery" to select two or three of their favorite paintings for "musical" inspiration.

Step 2a (using Garageband). Students write notes to describe their favorite painting using as many adjectives as possible. They then compose music using Garageband software to accompany the painting.

Step 2b (using classroom instruments). Arrange students together in small groups (two to four) based on favorite paintings. Using the available instruments, have the group discuss the painting and then compose music that is inspired by it.

Step 3. Groups perform their compositions for the class and report on their musical decisions based on the painting they used for inspiration.

Assessment: Are students able to:

✓ Compose music based on ideas inspired by an abstract painting?

✓ Describe the musical choices made for the composition?

Extensions and Variations:

• Create "liner" notes for the compositions.

• Work with the visual arts teacher and have students compose to other students' paintings or have students compose abstract music to inspire visual arts students' paintings.

Recordings and Other Resources:

• Allposters.com (http://www.allposters.com/) provides access to thousands of great art posters—either via a downloaded image or by purchasing a print.

• Feldman, M. (1971). *Rothko Chapel* [Recorded by California EAR Unit, William Winant, Deborah Dietrich, and David Abel] [Audio CD]. Tivoli, NY: New Albion Records (2009).

• McTee, C. (1993). Twittering Machine [Recorded by North Texas Wind Symphony]. On *Tributes* [Audio CD]. Boca Raton, FL: Klavier Music Productions (1995).

• Nordine, K. (1966). *Colors* [Audio CD]. San Francisco, CA: Asphodel Records (2000).

• Nordine, K. (2000). *Colors*. San Diego, CA: Harcourt Children's Books.

Form in Music

The composition must have a beginning, a middle, and an end; and it is up to the composer to see to it that the listener always has some sense of where he is in relation to beginning, middle, and end.

  AARON COPLAND, *What to Listen for in Music*

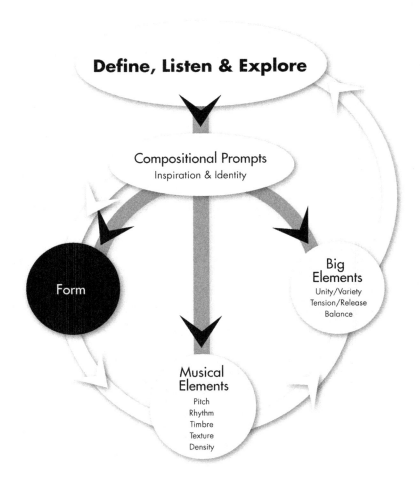

Form is the essence of everything. Everything we touch, see, and hear has a form to it. In music, like most temporal objects, the basic form is beginning, middle, and end. Often when I introduce the discussion of form in music composition with students, the issue is not *whether* a selection of music has a beginning, middle, and end, but whether or not, as Copland states in the opening quote, the listener knows where he or she is in relation to these parts. The most effective music uses the beginning to capture a listener's attention, the middle to keep a listener interested, and the ending to provide a complete and satisfying musical experience. So although it might be easy to explain to students that all music has a beginning, middle, and end, it is more challenging, and ultimately more educational, to have them compose with the purpose of making these sections musically effective.

At the most fundamental level, understanding form is the ability to differentiate *same* and *different* (repetition and contrast). Beyond repetition and contrast is the idea of development—that is, changing and extending what has been established. In successful beginnings, middles, and ends in music—as well as in stories, paintings, poetry, and so on—the concepts of repetition, contrast, and development are utilized effectively. An awareness of the basic ideas of repetition and contrast in form is innate and has been observed in children as young as 3 years old (Barrett, 1996; Flohr, 1985, 2005; McDonald & Simons, 1989; Moorhead & Pond, 1978/1951). And although children easily recognize the function of beginnings and endings, the idea of *middle* provides opportunities to help children learn how to develop musical ideas.

Because form is so ubiquitous and easy for everybody to understand, it presents the "next step" after inspiration and identity for teaching children to compose. The understanding of form through composition also makes a natural connection to other subjects such as literature, design, theater, film, and even science. This chapter will explore ideas for getting students to think about composing with effective form in music. We begin with beginnings and endings, and then move into ways in which the middle part might be filled. There are no absolute right ways to do this, but hopefully the suggested activities at the end of the chapter will provide some impetus for further ideas and music composition activities.

The Skeleton: Beginnings and Endings

Sometimes composers will talk about skeletons as an analogy for form—the skeleton is fleshed out to complete a music composition. Because skeletons can come in all shapes and sizes, teachers do not need to get caught up with teaching "real" forms (e.g., rondo, sonata-allegro form, ternary form) as the only forms. It is easy to forget that the historical forms we so often teach evolved and were labeled after the music was composed, and not the other way around. However, the forms we are most familiar with in classical music, such as rondo, or sonata-allegro form, can be useful skeletons for composing music. For students, thinking about form should begin with thinking about how to fill out a skeleton that makes sense to the listener, or to themselves as composers. So rather than talk about key, or measures, or riffs, or phrases, or specific forms, it may be more useful to think of the whole, and then filling in the parts. Composer Timothy Mahr, in explaining his own process of music composition offers this description:

> I try to establish a thread of connective thought that holds the piece together from start until finish. I call it the skeleton. At first it might just be a verbal description of what the piece will be. Then it becomes a flow chart of sorts, with shapes, diagrams, musical sketching, and a cobweb of lines drawn to show relationships and order. (Mahr, in Camphouse, 2002, p. 237)

I have found that working with children, beginnings and endings are a logical place to start when thinking about filling out a skeleton for a music composition.

Once Upon a Time . . .

It never fails that when I open a discussion with the question about what makes a good beginning to a story or book, one student will inevitably throw out the traditional "Once upon a time. . . ." This suggestion often prompts laughter that reflects an *"Aha!"* moment. A good beginning makes one wonder what is going to come next. Effective beginnings in fiction might catch the reader off guard; pose a question; present a problem or mystery; or simply introduce an important character by carefully describing the character to the reader.[1] Endings, on the other hand, put an end to the mystery, reveal the plot twist (sometimes with a surprise), or finish telling the story of the character introduced at the beginning. I've had many conversations with students about beginnings and endings in fiction and find that even the youngest can articulate why a story beginning and/or ending is effective or not. The similarities between literature and music beginnings and endings are quite obvious, and making this connection with students helps to guide the music composition process. Even the youngest student can take a simple classroom instrument and improvise an idea for a "mysterious" musical beginning.

When one begins to listen to some of the great classical music, we find there is no consistent or concrete "formula" for effective beginnings and endings. Successful beginnings in music might surprise the listener with a loud, percussive beginning (e.g., Beethoven's Symphony No. 7, *Allegretto* movement, or "O Fortuna" from Carl Orff's *Carmina Burana*) or present a quiet and mysterious motif that leaves the listener wondering how it will be answered or what will come next (e.g., Benjamin Britten's "Dawn" from *Four Sea Interludes from "Peter Grimes" Op. 33a*, Gustav Holst's "Mars" movement from the *Planets, Op. 32*, or Hector Berlioz "Marche au Supplice" from *Symphonie Fantastique*). Percussionist Evelyn Glennie, in her composition titled *Entrances* (which can be heard on the album *Evelyn Glennie: Her Greatest Hits*) really catches the listener off guard as it begins with the sound of footsteps approaching a microphone followed by the dialogue "Are you ready Phillip?"

Endings in music provide the resolution or answer to the mystery that was introduced. Again, these vary in great music just as they do in literature. A discussion of effective, or not so effective, endings in literature works well to parallel the idea in music. Students talk passionately about endings that leave them hanging and do not resolve the story. Often they'll break into a conversation about a common book they've read and agree upon the madness or brilliance of the way it ended. Music can finish with great force (again, Beethoven's Symphony No. 7, *Allegretto* movement) or fade away as quietly as it began (Britten's "Dawn" from *Four Sea Interludes from "Peter Grimes"*). Some endings are the same in force and volume as their beginnings (e.g., Carl Orff's "O Fortuna" from *Carmina Burana*) or are the opposite (e.g., compare the soft ostinato beginning of Holst's "Mars" from *The Planets* to the same movement's bombastic ending). Often some motif or musical idea that draws the listener's attention in the introduction is developed and comes to a satisfying conclusion.

When first approaching composition through form with students, I begin by asking the simple question stated earlier: What makes a good beginning, middle, and end in a story? We brainstorm and list the ideas for literature. After a discussion about what makes a good beginning and ending in fiction or even in a movie, I play short excerpts of musical beginnings and endings (such as those mentioned above) and ask them to describe the musical characteristics that seem to make them so effective. Outcomes of these discussions and exercises get students to understand that beginnings and endings, when done well, are effective devices in music just as they are in literature. They also learn that beginnings and endings can be similar or different, and there is really no "correct" method or formula to compose the ideal beginning and ending.

Another potential discussion to raise awareness of beginnings and endings is to talk about how, if beginnings and endings in music were different, a listener would know that they are from the same piece of music. What does a composer do to unite the beginning and ending? (Some potential answers: bring backs a motif or character, resolves or finishes an ostinato, resolves tension that was established at the beginning.) After discussion about the question of linking beginnings and endings and making connections to literature, we then go about composing beginnings and endings using the same tools we learned about in the exploration lessons: high/low, fast/slow, loud/soft, short/long, and different timbres. One parameter that I suggest for composing a beginning and/or ending is a time limit of 10 seconds. (See figure 5.1 as a sample guide for this first composition activity in form.)

There are several different variations and games that can be played when composing beginnings and endings. Groups of children can be divided and randomly assigned to compose a beginning or ending. The groups, after listening, then guess which was composed (beginning or ending) and then match beginnings and endings that work well together. A next task would be for the newly matched beginning and ending students to work together to create a middle section. Or assign pairs of children to work together—one to compose a beginning and one to compose a matching ending. To stretch skills even more, limit each

Beginnings...... middles ......ENDINGS

What do you know already? What do you hear? Use the table to think about good beginnings and endings in literature.

What about music? When you have good ideas, then compose a beginning and an ending!

	Beginning	Middle	Ending
Literature: List the characteristics that contribute to good beginnings, middle and endings of stories:			
Listen: What do you hear that makes these beginnings and endings effective? List these musical characteristics:			
Compose! Create a beginning and ending (no more than 10 seconds in length) that use some of the characteristics you describe above. Sketch your ideas in the boxes to help you organize and remember.			

FIGURE 5.1 Template for "Beginnings and Endings" Composition Activity

 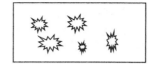 

FIGURE 5.2 **Sample Visual Blocks for Beginnings, Middles, and Endings Exercise**

student to use only two or three tools for composing their beginning or ending (e.g., high/low, fast/slow, loud/soft).

Another enjoyable activity is to connect visual shapes to beginnings, middles, and endings. How do random shapes look best when lined up? What do they sound like? Examine the three boxes in figure 5.2. How would they sound if played in that order? Might one box make a better beginning than the other? Which one, and why? Which makes the best beginning? Why? Which makes the best ending or middle, and why? Could you use the same one for both the beginning and ending? Ask students to compose music to various shapes such as those in figure 5.2 or ones they make up. Then have them decide whether their shapes sound best as a beginning or ending. Though there are virtually no right or wrong answers to these questions, students will certainly be drawn to think more sensitively when composing a beginning or ending.

Middles

After examining and composing with beginnings and endings, a natural next step is to talk about "middles." Fundamental to good middles are the ideas of repetition/contrast (same/different), and development or change. And here, too, there are clear analogies in literature, movies, and theater. At the most basic level, composers start with an idea and then do something with it. Something changes, develops, varies in the middle to keep the listener interested, and then resolves somehow to form a satisfying ending. An *idea* in music is a motif, analogous perhaps to a character in a good novel. "Every composer keeps in mind the possible metamorphoses of his succession of notes. First he tries to find its essential nature, and then he tries to find what might be done with it—how that essential nature may momentarily be changed" (Copland, 1985/1939, p. 25).

Paynter (1992) refers to using musical ideas as "growth points." This is helpful in getting students to think about making their musical ideas "grow" into something different. I have discovered that developing or changing initial musical ideas is one of the most difficult tasks for students to accomplish in the composition process. They are quick to compose an initial gesture and move on, but when asked to think about changing an idea or developing it to something more, they often need guidance and encouragement. The ability to actually develop a good idea is perhaps one of the most important skills of a successful, creative composer.

More structured assignments work best for getting students to think carefully and patiently about developing their musical ideas. In *Sound and Structure*, John Paynter (1992) provides several ideas for prompting composers to develop ideas. One simple assignment is to mess around with a fragment of music (a familiar tune or somebody's "beginning") and develop it into something different and more interesting. Another composition activity is to ask students to simply "Compose a short musical idea and do something with it." How might one create contrast using the parameters of high//low, soft/loud, fast/slow, short/long? To be even more structured in the approach, ask students to change just *one* note in some way. Then two notes, three notes, and so on. Listening to the minimalist works of Philip Glass, Terry Riley, Steve Reich, and György Ligeti could provide fodder for excellent discussion about development, or lack thereof, in music over time. The first movement of Ligeti's *Musica Ricercata* explores dynamics and timbres using only one note, until the very last note of the piece.

The concept of theme and variations provides an excellent tool for learning about changing musical ideas. (In chapter 3 I introduced the SCAMPER acronym as a device to aid students' creations of variations.) Mozart's 12 Variations on "Ah vous dirai-je maman," K.265, (familiar to us as variations on the children's melody "Twinkle Twinkle Little Star"), provides an excellent example of a very simple melody that is varied in recognizable ways in each of the subsequent variations. The basic forms of AABA and rondo also offer simple ways for getting children to develop, repeat, and contrast ideas, while at the same time learning about form in music.

In the performance ensemble setting, there are numerous pieces in the literature that students perform that provide examples of theme and variations, or at least show clear examples of the composer taking a theme and varying it. These techniques in the ensemble literature can be used as examples for students to take note of when learning a piece; students can then try their own variation on the theme or motif that the composer changed in the piece that they are performing.

The overall nature of sonata-allegro form, and its many variants, in classical music is perhaps one of the most familiar and successful forms in music and also provides a nice template for musical development. Paynter breaks down this "paradigm of some of the greatest musical forms" into the following simple bullets:

A Classical Structure
- An idea is established at some length.
- It is disturbed, ever so slightly, by something new.
- Development follows, materials move on with greater vigour in a series of short episodes to a high point of climax.
- This is followed by recapitulation of earlier material, modified to keep the progression alive.
- Then an extended, controlled relaxing of the tension.
- And finally a brief "reawakening" to emphasise and add strength to the final cadence. (Paynter, 1992, p. 191)

For more experienced student composers, this guide works well to help them create and develop their initial musical ideas. For younger students, this "classical form" can be simplified into simpler terms, such as in the following example:

- Create a short musical idea as a beginning.
- Repeat this idea but add to it and change it slightly. Do this at least three times.
- Add a musical surprise!
- Repeat your first musical idea.
- Add an ending to you music.

When having students compose a multimovement composition (often titled their "First Symphony"), I use Paynter's description of classical form for movements 1 and 4 and then describe movements 2 and 3 as they might appear in a typical symphony (see activity 5F in this chapter for more specifics). I've had children as young as 8 as well as adults write their first symphonies using this framework. They are delightfully surprised upon finishing a symphony and the mystery of this classical structure begins to be unveiled. It is also a simple and effective way to begin to understand form and why such forms are effective in the music we listen to everywhere. Song form is a form most common to many students, and I often move to song form assignments after this initial symphony assignment.

Conclusion

As the great composer Aaron Copland reminds us, a composer must let the listener know "where he is in relation to beginning, middle, and end" (1985/1939, p. 31). Working with the fundamental aspects of form follows the exploration, and then inspiration/identity, phase for beginning composers. All students can grasp the meaning of beginnings and endings, and as they mature they can work to craft the subtleties that make the most effective beginnings and endings in music. Form is related to the very important compositional element of development—a skill that requires more attention than many of the others. The consideration of development in form sometimes works best with guided, structured, or "closed" assignment parameters to compel students to develop initial music gestures.

As suggested earlier, provide a means for students to keep collections of their musical ideas so that they learn to try them more than once, to come back to ideas and change them for different musical compositions. This attitude and practice supports a *process*-based approach to music composition rather than a strictly *product*-based approach. Learning about and experimenting with form is one step of that process.

Composition Exercises

ACTIVITY 5A: Beginner: Same-Change-Different

Rationale:	Playing with same and different is a basic and simple technique that composers employ. This concept is easy for children to understand and is probably used in many classes outside of music. This musical game of "same-change-different" is a fun way for students to become skilled at creating variations on themes—albeit very simple at the start.
Level/Type:	Beginning. Groups of three or four.
Materials:	Bell sets (or any melodic musical instrument such as keyboards)
Objectives:	Students will: • Change an existing short musical motive to compose something new • Compose their own musical motive for others to change
Length:	One class period
Preparation:	Begin class with the students in a large circle, each with a bell set to use. They will go around the circle starting with a short (3- or 4-note) motive that will be passed clockwise around the circle from player to player. A player receives it, plays it as he or she hears it, and then changes it by altering either one note or the rhythm. This becomes the new motive for the next person to change and pass on. Talk about how composers often take a musical idea and change it. Listen to Mozart's 12 Variations on "Ah vous dirai-je maman" ("Twinkle, Twinkle Little Star" is the theme), and have students draw graphic pictures to illustrate each variation. (For older children, one might use the "Greeting Prelude"—a variation on "Happy Birthday" by Stravinsky.) List the ways that the variations changed the melody on a class board.
Procedures:	Step 1. Assign students into groups of three or four. They are essentially to follow the same procedure as the circle warm-up activity but within their own group. Provide each group with paper and markers. Instructions: *In your group, come up first with a simple musical idea that you all can play together. Then as a group work on three different variations of the idea that you can play together. Finish your composition with the first idea. Draw a picture to represent your musical idea and its variations* (the notation is optional if there is time).

Step 2. Students practice together on their "theme and variations."

Step 3. Students will perform for the class, explaining their variations and the drawings that accompany these.

Assessment: Are students able to:

    ✓ Compose a simple theme in a group?

    ✓ Create three variations to a simple theme?

    ✓ Graphically represent their theme and variations?

Extensions and   • This exercise could be used with just rhythm instruments.
Variations:
    • Have students create variations to simple tunes they are learning in class.

Recordings and   • Mozart, W. A. (c. 1781). 12 Variations on "Ah vous dirai-je maman,"
Other   K.265 [Recorded by John Novacek]. On *Great Mozart Piano Works*
Resources: [Audio CD]. Palatine, IL: Four Winds Entertainment (2000).

    • Stravinsky, I. (1955). Greeting Prelude [Recorded by the London Symphony Orchestra]. On *Stravinsky in America* [Audio CD]. New York: RCA Records (1997).

ACTIVITY 5B: Intermediate: Beginnings and Endings and in Between

Rationale: Everybody understandings the concept of starting and stopping. What does this sound like in music? What makes a good beginning or ending in music or in fiction or in a movie? This activity allows for a variety of options for composing and sensitizes the composers to crafting "good" beginnings and endings in music. It offers many options for extensions by examining "middles" in music and thinking about development or other forms.

Level/Type: Beginning composers of any age. Groups of two or three students.

Materials:
- Miscellaneous classroom instruments (or any objects that make sounds)
- Recordings: choose from a variety of music that offers effective and different beginnings and endings (see excerpts mentioned earlier in this chapter). The theme "2001: A Space Odyssey" (also known as Richard Strauss's *Also sprach Zarathustra, Op. 30*) is a great example because it begins with one long held-out note. Simple but extremely effective.

Objectives: Students will:
- Describe effective beginnings and endings in music using terms such as mysterious, unknown, tension, impact (beginnings); complete, relieved, repeated notes, release (endings)
- Compose short beginning and ending excerpts based on descriptions

Length: One to two class periods

Preparation: Prompt a discussion about beginnings and endings in stories and in movies. Instructions: *Remember the story we just read? How did it begin? How did it end? How did we know it was over? Was the beginning good? Why? What did the author do at the beginning to make it interesting? Composers in music use these same procedures to create beginnings and endings in music. Write down the characteristics that describe good story beginnings and endings.*

Procedures: Introduction: *We are going to listen to music that has very interesting beginnings and endings. See if you can hear how the composer makes the musical sounds interesting. Then we will compose musical beginnings and endings.* Play musical excerpts, and have students describe their listening observations on a worksheet.

Step 1. Listen. Play 5–10 seconds of the beginnings and endings of a variety of excerpts (see resources listed at end of lesson). Give students time to write impressions between each excerpt.

Step 2. Discussion. Discuss the excerpts with students. See what they wrote down for descriptions. Provide excerpts that have different musical characteristics so that students will not be able to uniformly pick common *musical* characteristics (such as "all beginnings are soft" or "all beginnings are loud").

Optional discussion: How do we know that the beginning and ending excerpts belong together? Discussion should lead to the idea that the composer uses mostly the same instruments in both and often repeats an idea in both—whether it is a simple rhythm or a complete motive.

Step 3. Divide the students into groups of two or three. Assign each group to either compose a beginning and matching ending *or* assign each group to compose *either* a beginning or ending. (Then when they are finished, others can try to guess which each group composed, and also try to match beginnings and endings that complement each other.)

Using any combination of your musical instruments, work together to compose a short beginning [ending]. Think of the characteristics we came up with to describe good beginnings and endings and try to include these in your composition. Your beginning and/or ending should not be longer than 10 seconds. [If composing both a beginning and an ending: your beginning and ending should share at least one common feature.] Practice it several times so that you can perform it for the class.

Step 4. Perform the beginnings and endings (ask performers to place about 5 seconds of silence in between the beginning and ending if they are performing both). Discuss as appropriate and time allows (i.e., have performers explain their compositions; ask audience members to critique based on the characteristics used to describe these). Guess the beginnings and endings if this option was used. If groups composed both a beginning and an ending, discuss how they were similar.

Assessment: Are students able to:

✓ Portray characteristics of effective beginnings and endings in their original composition?

✓ Compose a beginning and ending that contains a common feature (motif, rhythm, timbre, instrumentation, etc.)?

Extensions and
Variations:

- Match beginnings and endings from different groups. Then have the groups work together to create a middle and transitions to connect the beginning, middle and endings.
- Create multiple sections (such as ABACADA).
- Pair up students to improvise a musical conversation that begins and then must end. (How do you initiate? How do you indicate the conversation is ended? Record and analyze for musical structure.)

Recordings and
Other
Resources:

- Beethoven, L. (1811). Symphony No. 7, Allegretto movement, Op. 92. On *Bernstein: The Final Concert* [Audio CD]. Berlin: Deutsche Grammophon (1992).
- Berlioz, H. (1855). Marche au supplice from *Symphonie fantastique* [Recorded by the San Francisco Symphony]. On *Berlioz: Symphonie fantastique* [Audio CD]. New York: RCA (2004).
- Britten, B. (1945). "Dawn" from Four Sea Interludes from *Peter Grimes* [Recorded by the Boston Symphony Orchestra]. On *Bernstein: The Final Concert* [Audio CD]. Berlin: Deutsche Grammophon (1992).
- Glennie, E. (1994). Entrances. On *Evelyn Glennie: Her Greatest Hits* [Audio CD]. New York: RCA (1998).
- Holst, G. (1916). Mars Movement from the *Planets, Op. 32* [Recorded by the Montreal Symphony Orchestra]. On *Holst: The Planets* [Audio CD]. London: Decca (2007).
- Orff, C. (1936). O Fortuna from *Carmina Burana* [Recorded by the Cleveland Orchestra & Chorus]. On *Orff: Carmina Burana* [Audio CD]. New York: Sony (2005 remastered).
- Strauss, R. (1896). 2001: A Space Odyssey (Also sprach Zarathustra) [Recorded by the City of Prague Philharmonic Orchestra]. On *The Incredible Film Music Box* [Audio CD]. New York: Silva Screen Records (2005).

ACTIVITY 5C: Advanced: Song Form

Rationale: Song form is perhaps the most common form known to students, as it is prevalent in popular music. Song writing is a valued skill and can also be therapeutic for adolescent students because they can tell stories of their own lives. Although there is not one single correct song form, this lesson will start with the premise that *all* songs have some combination of verse and repeating chorus structure.

Level/Type: This lesson assumes that students' basic chord progression knowledge is already in place. Students will also need a working knowledge of an accompaniment instrument: guitar, piano, or mallet instrument.

Materials: • Accompaniment instrument such as piano keyboard, guitar, mallet instrument, or Autoharp
                • Paper and writing tools

Objectives: Students will:
                • Compose a song using a structure from those given
                • Notate the lyrics and chord progression of the song
                • Perform their song (or teach it to another person to perform)

Length: Three to four class periods

Preparation: Introduce the song form concept by sharing lyrics from various songs (examples given below). Have students work to figure out the form of pop songs by writing lyrics to their favorite songs and seeing that most songs have a verse and repeated chorus structure.

Procedures: Step 1. After "discovering" various song form structures from writing lyrics to favorite pop songs, show the chart of five possible structures:

#1	#2	#3	#4	#5
A Verse	A Verse	A Chorus	A Verse	A Verse
B Chorus	B Chorus	B Verse	A Verse	A Verse
A Verse	A Verse	A Chorus	B Chorus	A Verse
B Chorus	B Chorus	B Verse	A Verse	A Verse
A Verse	C Bridge	A Chorus	A Verse	
B Chorus	B Chorus		B Chorus	

Step 2. Listen to pop songs that depict some of these different structures. Have students follow the lyrics as the song is playing, and try to identify the structure. Examples might include *Walking the Dog* by Rufus Thomas (#2 from the chart above); *The Times They Are a-Changin'* by Bob Dylan (#5 from chart above).

Step 3. Have students work in pairs to come up with original lyrics following one of the structures in the chart.

Step 4. Have students work together to put the lyrics to a melody that they can remember. Then they add a basic chord progression to their melody (one student might sing, while the other accompanies either on guitar, piano, or mallet instrument).

Step 5. Students share songs with class.

Assessment:	Are students able to: ✓ Compose and perform song following one of the five form options? ✓ Compose and perform a song with basic chord accompaniment?
Extensions and Variations:	• Students could work with a program such as Band-in-a-Box or GarageBand to create accompaniments to their songs.
Recordings and Other Resources:	• Dylan, B. (1963). The Times They Are a-Changin'. On *Bob Dylan's Greatest Hits, Vol. 1* [Audio CD]. New York: Sony Music Entertainment (2000). • Thomas, R. (1963). Walking the Dog. On *Garfield: The Movie* [Audio CD]. New York: Rhino/Rykodisc (2004).

ACTIVITY 5D: Technology: Building Blocks

Rationale: The proliferation of new (inexpensive and sometimes free) technology
                    software has opened up wonderful possibilities for creating music.
                    "Looping" software such as GarageBand allows users to combine
                    loops of premade music excerpts that makes them sound like they
                    belong together. If one does not have access to Apple computers and
                    GarageBand, the free online program Soundation (http:// soundation
                    .com/) provides a platform for looping compositions. One could also
                    use the free sound editing program Audacity by uploading preexist-
                    ing loops for students to manipulate. The idea in this assignment is
                    to provide music building blocks for students to manipulate in order
                    to compose a composition of a desired form. In the following
                    exercise, a simple introduction, AABA middle, and ending are
                    required; however, the technology is such that teachers could
                    work in any form.

Level/Type: Beginning–intermediate. Individual or groups.

Materials: • Computer with music looping or sound editing software (e.g.,
                      GarageBand)
                    • Headphones

Objectives: Students will:
                    • Select and combine preexisting sound loops to compose music in
                      AABA form (or another form designated by the teacher).

Length: One class period

Preparation: The software should be preorganized with a limited number of pre-
                    existing musical "blocks" from which students can choose (these can
                    be any length and any style). Students at this point should under-
                    stand the basics of dragging and dropping music blocks onto
                    multiple tracks.

Procedures: Introduction: Provide students with the instructions to work out an
                    original piece of music that has an introduction, AABA form in the
                    middle, and an ending. Give them the choices of the limited sets
                    of musical blocks so that they have to make strategic decisions for
                    putting these in an order. Encourage them to add dynamics to the
                    music before finishing (e.g., fade out for ending).
                    Step 1. Students work on creating their music.
                    Step 2. If there is time, students perform their music for their
                    classmates.

Assessment: Are students able to:

✓ Compose music, using preexisting musical blocks, into a form that has an introduction, AABA middle, and ending?

✓ Manipulate the software to add expressive elements to the music?

Extensions and Variations:

- Have students create musical blocks of their own and trade with others to compose an original composition.
- Break up several preexisting digital song files into sound blocks and have students remix the blocks into a new and original composition.

ACTIVITY 5E: Ensemble: SCAMPER

Rationale: One way to really understand a music composition is to begin to understand the techniques a composer used to create the composition. In a performance ensemble, this way of understanding can enhance a student's musical experience as a performer. Composing short excerpts using the technique of the composer is even better and perhaps the easiest form to understand and then try this out in an ensemble setting is theme and variations. In *Rejouissance* by James Curnow, the theme from "A Mighty Fortress Is Our God" is manipulated and varied in several ways, sometimes it is hard to even recognize. Using the SCAMPER technique (see below), have students mess with this same theme and come up with ways to vary it. See if any of them had the same idea that Curnow did. Even though the following lesson is linked to one particular composition, the ideas can easily be transferred to any ensemble composition that uses theme and variations.

Level/Type: Beginning composer/intermediate-level concert band.

Materials:
• *Rejouissance* for concert band by James Curnow
• Score paper, manuscript paper, and pencils

Objectives: Students will:
• Write a variation on the theme from *Rejouissance*
• Describe the variation technique they used to vary the theme
• Identify places in *Rejouissance* where the composer varied the theme.

Length: One concert season

Preparation: When first reading *Rejouissance*, provide the band with a brief explanation of the techniques that Curnow uses: that is to vary in several ways the theme from "A Mighty Fortress."

Procedures: Step 1. Hand out copies of the "Mighty Fortress" theme to all members of the band, and use it as a warm-up so students can become familiar with the theme (see figure 5.D.1):

Step 2. Provide manuscript paper to students with the instructions to vary the theme using one of the "SCAMPER" possibilities (see figure 3.1 for the SCAMPER chart). The resulting variation should be written clearly in standard notation, and they should be able to perform it.

Step 3. Collect compositions, and use them as sight-reading warm-ups on rehearsal days. Discuss the variations and the techniques students used.

Assessment:

Are students able to:

✓ Compose one variation to the theme "A Mighty Fortress" from *Rejouissance* using a SCAMPER technique?

✓ Articulate the technique used to create their variation?

✓ Write their variation in standard notation clearly enough that they or any other performer can read and perform it?

Extensions and Variations:

• Provide students with access to the full score for *Rejouissance*, and ask them to find at least one place in the score where the theme is varied. Highlight the different variation techniques that Curnow used, and then have the students create their own in a similar manner.

• Highlight student variations at an "informance" concert of *Rejouissance*—linking specific variations by students that are similar to style in variations Curnow uses in the music.

Recordings and Other Resources:

• Curnow, J. (1987). *Rejouissance Concert Band Music*. Winona, MN: Hal Leonard.

ACTIVITY 5F: Multimovement Composition

Rationale: The purpose of this assignment is to bring together many small ideas for students to compose their first multimovement (sometimes I call it their first *symphony*) composition. This brings form up to a "meta level," such that now the composers need to think not only about form for a single movement or piece, but how form overall can link several movements together. This works for composers of any age, but it is best as a culminating activity when students have progressed through and tried many other types of composition activities.

Level/Type: All levels after some experience with other composition activities.

Materials: Any musical instruments or technology

Length: Several days

Procedures: Listen to a variety of classical multimovement symphonies with students to share with them the sense of how each movement is structured (in a very global sense) as well as how the movements seem to fit together. Instructions: *Create a "Sound Symphony" that follows the movement forms and descriptions below. Think of a unifying element to tie the entire four movements together. This can be anything (e.g., a theme, a motif, a key, a rhythm, a story). Whatever unifying device you use, it should help to make your multimovement composition sound like the four movements belong together. Include descriptions/thoughts/reflections for each movement. Describe the "unifying" device that you used to tie your four movements together. Turn in your reflective comments with your assignment.*

- Movement I: Follow a "Classical" structure. (See the description of a "Classical" structure earlier in this chapter).
- Movement II: Slow and soft (e.g., a pretty melody with chords or just slow and mysterious sounds)
- Movement III: Quick and light, dance-like
- Movement IV: Much like first movement "Classical" structure but with a "twist" for a grand ending!—build to a loud ending

Assessment: Are students able to:
                 ✓ Compose a multimovement composition following the forms/ structure outlined for each movement?

✓ Use and articulate their use of a unifying device that ties the symphony together?

✓ Describe their musical choices for each movement?

Extensions and Variations:

This multimovement composition can be notated, if that is the goal, for a standard ensemble, or created using technology. The variations as to the kind of ensemble or performance medium that it is composed for are limitless.

Musical Elements

Composing music is one of the most painless and stimulating ways of learning to understand how music works.

J. HOWARD, *Learning to Compose*

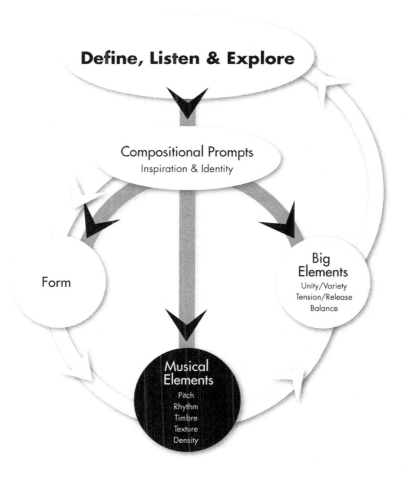

What are you going to teach today? Teach it through music composition! Although learning about the traditional musical elements is considered a basic part of any music education, having students learn about the musical elements through composing is perhaps the most successful way to teach *and* to assess whether they've learned. In this chapter, I will examine the more technical details of composing—that is, composing with more parameters in order to develop technical facility with the "parts" of music. Whereas the beginning of the suggested composition curriculum in this book starts with fewer parameters and more exploration, this phase moves to specific, more "rule-bound" composition activities in order to *learn about* the parts that make the whole. The goal with these activities is to learn more about the techniques of composition through learning about the musical elements.

But first, a brief note about "musical elements." I use the phrase *musical elements* to talk about the different parts of music. Oftentimes we take for granted that the musical elements are the five commonly learned in elementary school: melody, harmony, rhythm, texture, and timbre (or some similar combination). Aside from the fact that these "musical elements" come in different variations, I would suggest that the ones we tend to use in "school music" are not ubiquitous to all music. For instance, *melody* is a subcategory of *pitch*, and though all music has some element of pitch, much of the of the world's music does not contain a melody (at least when we think of melodies in the Western European tradition). *Harmony* implies a chord structure or system, whereas *pitch*, when aligned vertically, is the same thing—whether harmonious or not. In an intriguing article, Rob Cutietta challenges music educators to think about describing musical elements in the way music is *perceived* rather than the way they have typically been using them. He specifically suggests using words such as *motion, energy, flow, fabric,* and *color* as alternatives to the musical elements (Cutietta, 1993). It doesn't necessarily matter how the musical elements are broken down, or what they are called, only that teachers are sensitive to the fact that some of the element labels are unique to only certain traditions of music. Although a word such as *melody* is useful when teaching within certain musical traditions, I feel it is more useful to use musical element labels that work for *all* music when composing. For this chapter I will use the following list of terms as the musical elements, along with some of the traditional ones we use:

- Pitch: single or in combination (harmony)
- Rhythm: timing and duration (including articulation)
- Timbre: sound "colors"
- Texture: pitches combined in various ways and articulations
- Density: thickness or thinness of sounds, volume

As mentioned previously, rather than starting with specifics, it is better to begin in exploration and later move into the details, such as will be presented in this chapter. One outcome of the exploration stage is to create a "need to know" disposition in students that will create curiosity for more technical learning. However there is a myth (often manifest in the fear of composing too early) that students need the technical *before* the exploration, that students need rules first before they can compose.

An example of the apprehension of composing before learning the technical details is illustrated through a conversation I had with an elementary music teacher. Jeannie had graciously agreed to let one of my college students present a composition lesson to her second-grade music class. When my student told Jeannie that her lesson would involve having the children compose beginnings and endings to melodies using bell sets, Jeannie cautioned, "But the children haven't learned their scales yet, nor do they understand time signatures." (They had not composed music before either.) The lesson that my student wanted to teach sounded much too complicated to Jeannie, when, in fact, the student teacher was simply going to introduce the idea of beginning melodic gestures (going up) and ending melodic gestures (going down). The lesson was uncomplicated and took only 20 minutes. After a brief introduction that involved modeling pitches going up and then going down, children, paired together with bell sets, took turns to create a beginning (something that goes up) and an ending (notes that go down) to make their short melody. The young students not only understood the assignment without having prior knowledge of scales or time signatures, but they enjoyed it and it resulted in a basic conceptual understanding of up and down in music, as well as beginnings and endings. This foundation will aid students when they *do* begin to learn more specifically the role of key signatures in music.

The lesson involved no wrong notes, no strict key or time signature, just an early introduction to a concept that gave students the power to immediately create and at the same time demonstrate a basic understanding. (An unintended outcome of the lesson became obvious when some children needed to ask which way on the bell sets made notes go higher.) As students progress through lessons about scales and time signatures in subsequent years, then the lesson on beginnings and endings can be repeated but with more technical terms and parameters. And so it should go through an upward spiral of learning about music *through* composing; there is no need to wait until some of the so-called basics are learned first.

A great myth about music composition is that one must learn technical rules before doing any "real" music composition. On the contrary, the most powerful learning will occur when children are allowed to create in order to learn the rules. The musical elements of pitch, rhythm, timbre, texture, and density provide the perfect scaffolding to learn about the craft of music through music composition.

Composing to learn about music can apply as easily to a performance ensemble classroom as it does to a general music classroom. In the ensemble classroom, use the music that is being performed as the stimulus for a composition activity. Students will learn more about the music they are performing as a result. Examine musical scores for potential composing/teaching opportunities related to melody, rhythm, harmony, timbre, or texture. When doing an analysis of a score, ask, "What about each of the music elements might lend itself to a composition activity?" and "What compositional technique did the composer use that might be easy for my students to try?" The answers to these questions may provide ideas for simple composition exercises in a performance ensemble.

A Composition Exercise for the Band

An example of a composition activity on melody writing that I have used in a band setting was inspired by the melody to John Paulson's *Epinicion* (1975). *Epinicion* is a level 5 band composition that uses one theme repeatedly throughout. Behind the haunting theme is a growing cacophony of aleatoric sounds that build to a loud climax. The ending is a poignant, soft, and fading repetition of the main theme, played by piccolo and alto clarinet. Paulson uses mostly tritones and half steps to formulate this theme (see figure 6.1). A composition assignment for students in the ensemble, as they are rehearsing this work, is to write a melody using only 2 intervals. Two rules would follow: (1) make the melody approximately the same length as the theme in *Epinicion*, and (2) be able to play it on your instrument. (This can be taken further by composing an entire band piece in the style of *Epinicion*. The process for doing this is outlined in activity 7E in chapter 7.)

This relatively simple lesson takes very little time away from rehearsal and provides students not only with the opportunity to learn some basic music theory (intervals) but also to exercise creative thinking through melody writing while gaining knowledge about the music they are rehearsing and will ultimately perform. Even if one composition activity per year (such as this simple example) were to take place in an ensemble setting, students would benefit.

When composing around the musical elements, there are two caveats to keep in mind. First, there is no music that exists with only one of the musical elements—the elements are artificial concepts that we use in order to be able to talk about and dissect music. In other words, a melody doesn't exist without rhythm and timbre, rhythm also contains timbre, harmony implies texture and density and pitch, texture combines melody, harmony and rhythm, and so on. Too often we get caught teaching concepts in music (the parts) and forget that these parts always intertwine into an aesthetic whole. Second, it is important to remember that any "technical" composition activities should continuously be supplemented with varied and rich musical listening in order to continuously expose students to the vast variety of music as it exists with all of the musical elements combined—in other words, do not sacrifice the richness of music while getting into details and techniques.

In the remainder of this chapter I offer composition ideas for several of the music elements, first by discussing the conceptual basis of each element, and then providing a sample of composition activities that one might use when teaching about the elements.

FIGURE 6.1 Main Theme from Epinicion

Pitch

In the most basic scientific explanation, pitches in music are the frequencies of vibration that we hear. In Western music traditions, pitch is organized around 12 major and 12 minor scales, and a coherent series of pitches in a row is called a melody. When pitches are arranged vertically, and within the system of scales, it is called harmony. Following are some examples of learning about melody and harmony through music composition.

Melody

I present the following definition for melody when working with students:

> A melody is a series of musical notes that are memorable and sound like they belong together. A home tone in the melody makes it sound final.

This basic definition can eventually lead to the more technical concepts of tonic, dominant, and the other more complicated harmonic implications that are in place for a "good" melody.[1] I have found this definition to work well with even the youngest of students, and it provides a basis for all the other concepts one might teach about melody as students' sophistication grows through music classes, lessons, and experience. Other concepts to be learned about melody include the ideas that melodies have contour (up and down) and often contain a variety of steps, leaps, and repeated notes. Altering any of these can have a profound effect on a melody. Questions to trigger experimentation with melody building with students might include the following: What if a melody was made of only leaps? Only steps? Only repeated notes? What is the best combination of these? All melodies have rhythm and some melodies are symmetrical—that is, they are balanced into equal phrases.

With each of the melodic concepts described above one can imagine any number of simple composition exercises for students to learn about the concept being taught. (Activity 6A at the end of this chapter provides an example of one of the first melody assignments that I give to students.) Following are a few other ideas for teaching composition around the basic concepts of melody. Remember, there are as many possibilities for melody composition as there are concepts to be taught about melody!

Playing with Contour

One can imagine several variations of creating melodies with contours in mind. For instance, a student might try to match a classmate's composed melody with another melody of a similar contour. Teachers can provide a melody for students to draw the contour, or have students draw a contour from which others are to compose. It is important to remember that for first-time attempts, there are no right or wrong notes—it is about simply introducing the idea of contour and seeing whether students understand the concept by being able to put together a series of notes to match a visual or aural contour. As students get

more sophisticated in their melody writing, then they might experiment with
tonic-dominant-tonic relationships within
the melody. The following exercise has
students create melodies that follow a
contour.

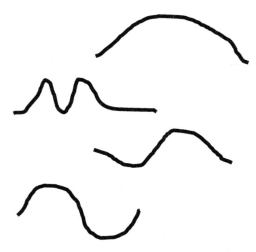

1. Create a relatively simple and short
   melody on a bell set (or keyboard)
   that uses one of the 4 contours shown
   in figure 6.2.
2. Practice your melody several times so
   that you can remember it.
3. Prepare to perform your melody for
   class.

FIGURE 6.2 Contours for Melody Composition

4. Classmates will listen to your performance and try to determine which contour you
   chose for your melody.

Guaranteed to Sound Good

The following exercise results in a pretty "good" sounding melody—it is cohesive and
forms a nice, symmetrical 8-measure melody. A springboard from this exercise would be to
teach about tonic/dominant relationships in a melody; or have students change the rhythm
slightly to hear the effect this has.

1. In a treble clef staff, create a simple 2-measure melody (use only eighth, quarter, and/or
   half notes). You may include rests.
2. In the next 2 measures (measures 3–4), use the same rhythm of the first melody, but use
   different notes.
3. Repeat step 2 for measures 5–6 and 7–8. Make sure that the last note in the entire
   8-measure melody is the same as the first note of the song.

Harmony

Harmony happens when two or more pitches sound at the same time. It is common to view
harmony as something that accompanies (or is secondary) to a melody. The most commonly taught concept of harmony lies within the Western musical canon: that is, music
basically moves from a tonic through a subdominant, eventually a dominant, and, at some
point, back to a tonic. There are, of course, several music texts that outline the rules that
one must follow in order to create and understand this "common practice" harmony. It is
not uncommon in our traditional university musical training to drill the rules of proper
harmony writing, sometimes devoid of sound, and often to the detriment of exploration.

Perhaps it is because of this training that the thought of teaching *about* harmony to young children—especially through composition—seems very advanced. Yet if we go back to the idea that harmony is simply two or more pitches sounding at the same time, we can teach *anybody* about music harmony through composition, even the very youngest children. Which two notes sound good together? Which do not? How does a chord sound compared to a cluster (never mind which chord or which cluster)? Once again, in composition, we need to forget the "rules" and begin by allowing students to explore and discover the sounds that different harmonies produce.

When introducing the concept of chordal harmony to young students, I first explore the sounds of clusters and consonant triads. For students who understand notation, I begin by showing on a staff how a 3-note chord is built (all lines, or all spaces). Every note has a possibility of at least creating three different chords. For example, an A could be the bottom of an A chord, the 3rd of an F chord, or the fifth of a D chord. With each example, I play the chord on the piano (notation should *always* be accompanied with sound). Then we might explore several chordal possibilities before sending students off to figure out "good-sounding" chord progressions on barred instruments or keyboards. The following is an example of a first composition assignment I give that introduces concepts in chordal harmony.

"Beautiful Chords"

At this point the students understand that a chord contains three simultaneous notes that are separated by a note.

- Materials: mallet instruments or keyboards; manuscript paper and pencil.
- Students work in pairs (if on a mallet instrument, then one student has one mallet and the other student has two mallets).
- Procedure:
  1. Explore a variety of chords on your instrument.
  2. Find a series of 6 chords in a row that sound good.
  3. Carefully notate these chords.
  4. Practice playing these chords in a slow, steady manner.
  5. Be prepared to play your "Beautiful Chord" sequence for class.

There are, of course, several variations for this assignment: repeat chords, roll chords, arpeggiate chords, trade notations and play each others' chord sequences, and so on.

A next step might be to add a melodic line to the chord sequence. One exercise that works very well for melody building on top of a chord progression is to follow a simple rule: when building a melody over chord tones, the first note of each measure should be one of the chord tones on that beat. Limit the rhythm to quarter notes and eighth notes, and the result is often a nice melody accompanied by a whole note chord sequence. (See activity 6D as an exercise for adding melodies to existing harmonies.)

A "backward" approach to this, and a nice way to segue from melody writing to harmony writing, is to begin with a melody that students have written, and then add harmony. This is illustrated in the following lesson.

Add Harmony to Your Melody

- Materials: keyboard or mallet instruments; manuscript paper and pencil.
- This lesson is most successful when students work in pairs.
- Procedure:
  1. Write a simple 4-measure melody using standard notation (or start with an existing simple melody).
  2. Use only whole, half, quarter, or eighth notes and rests in your melody.
  3. In each measure, draw the three possible chords that would fit with the first note of the melody in that measure. Sketch these chord possibilities below in an accompaniment staff.
  4. Explore your melody with each of the 3 chord options.
  5. Decide upon the best chord option for each measure, and circle it.
  6. Now fill in the accompaniment staff with your chords.

Two logical steps that might follow this exercise are to arpeggiate the chords or make an interesting rhythm with the chord tones. This exercise really requires exploration and careful listening in order to find the best sounds and chord sequences. Oftentimes the chord sequences and melodies that follow end up using the "rules" of Western tonal harmony and then provide a jumping-off point for teaching the theory behind the sound.

Computer notation software works especially well when teaching harmony because students receive immediate aural feedback when they move chords and notes around. There are now free web-based programs or inexpensive notation software that does not require MIDI keyboards. An example of such an exercise is to provide students with a template using notation software that has a melody line and a piano accompaniment line. Provide any 5 different chords at the start. The object is for students to copy and paste these chords into an 8-measure sequence that already has a simple melody. The exercise is more fully described in activity 6D.

All of the exercises described here teach students, through their own creative and aesthetic decision making, about "rules" of harmony and chord structure. Interestingly, I have realized that most students eventually end these creative harmony exercises on a tonic. From this kind of aural discovery, I then teach about the concept of tonic, dominant, leading chords, and so forth. Regardless of medium, the point of introducing the concept of harmony through composing is to get students to learn by using their ears. From that point we can teach them all the rules they need (or care) to know.

Rhythm

Virtually *any* rhythmic concept that is being taught can be turned into a composition exercise for deeper learning, as well as fun. Introducing 6/8 time? Make up a composition exercise that requires 6/8 time. When creating composition exercises to teach about a concept, keep the exercises short and simple, related to the concept, and include clear directions and parameters. If an assignment is too complex, the concept may become less focused. The following exercise could be used with students who are learning about 6/8 time shortly after it has been introduced (this would also work well with students in a beginning instrumental program when they first stumble on 6/8 time in their method books).

6/8 March Composition

- Materials: rhythm sticks; manuscript paper—with only one staff line and 4 measures demarcated; pencil.
- Procedure:
    1. Compose a 4-measure rhythm in 6/8 time.
    2. Use only quarter, eighth, and dotted quarter notes, and each at least one time.
    3. Make your rhythm sound like a march.
    4. Notate your rhythm on the paper provided.
    5. Practice your rhythm on your rhythm sticks, and be prepared to play your rhythm for class.

A variation is for students to trade their rhythm marches with one another and perform them for the class, hence emphasizing the need for good notation and reading skills.

Many would agree that the pop music culture within recent years has evolved to a more rhythmic than melodic focus. Rap and hip-hop music seem ubiquitous on students' iPods. Why not take advantage of this? Composing rap tunes and "beats" are obvious places to begin. As teachers we may feel a little "out of it" when it comes to knowing how to teach this, which makes for a perfect reason to have students teach *us*. With composition exercises centered around looped rhythmic beats, one can still teach all of the concepts about rhythm that would be taught through any other genre: fast/slow, steady beat, short/long, time signature, duple/triple, simple/compound, and so on. Whereas in a traditional method of teaching music, one might teach rhythmic concepts isolated from context, or connected to music that does not connect to students' lives, having students compose in a style they understand (such as hip-hop beats) will reinforce the concepts in a potentially more powerful and lasting way.

Beats

As I've grown to learn more about "beats" in hip-hop, I have acquired real respect for the composers who create them. A "beat," I have learned, is a small unit (often with melodic as well as rhythmic elements) that is looped repeatedly to form the basis for a hip-hop or rap piece.[2] I have observed young people sit for hours at a computer station working out their "beats" with careful precision and concentration. They proudly share their beats with each other and trade beats for composition foundations. Working with students in urban settings, I have learned that they are extremely meticulous when trying to mix just the right beat to go with a rap lyric they created. Students' ability to discriminate between the subtle differences in hip-hop beats never ceases to amaze me. Whereas one "beat" might sound as good as, or even the same as another to me, these students will not be satisfied until the exact bass drum sound (for instance) is found.

I have also learned that although some students prefer writing lyrics instead of beats, others consider themselves beat artists and not rappers (lyric writers). There is a culture of "beat artists" out there, and there are hundreds of websites where one can download beats for music making or manipulation. The students I have worked with know well, and can discriminate among, thousands of different beats. We would be foolish to ignore this expertise when it comes to teaching rhythmic concepts.

The Apple software program GarageBand and its Windows-equivalent Acid provide hundreds of premade beats and rhythmic/harmonic loops. Using these programs, students can paste loops together to create a composition. Although this might take the originality out of creating their own loops, it still provides a "drawing board" for their compositional imagination and a stepping stone to creating their own beats. Teachers can use these programs and then highlight the rhythmic concepts to be taught that exist in the materials being used to compose.

An example of a composition exercise in the rap genre would be to have students, working alone or in small groups, compose a variety of rhythmic beats. Parameters could be given in order to reinforce a concept, or, after the beats are composed, the concepts used could be highlighted and then explained (e.g., duple and triple meters, or half-, quarter-, eighth-, and sixteenth-note divisions). Beats from different students or groups could be combined to create one large composition (a lesson in form enters here). Add lyrics, and eventually an entire piece composed in song form, created with a variety of beats, results as a collaborative process between several students. Although a variety of computer software programs make beat composing really fun, no fancy equipment is necessarily needed because rhythm beats can be made with any object that makes noise.

Ideas for rhythm composition exercises are, of course, endless. Variations can include individual, pairs, groups of students; types of instruments; sharing and trading compositions; performing composition, and so on. What is the goal? If it is to teach a rhythmic concept *and* enhance understanding of this concept, then have students compose to learn the concept. Learning standard music notation (and creating the need to know standard music notation) also works well within simple rhythmic composition exercises.

Timbre

Timbre is to music what aroma is to food and color is to painting. It is the taste of music and perhaps the one element in music that encompasses all others. Timbre contributes a visceral experience to the aural in music that makes each listening experience unique. It can be as pure as a boy soprano or as heavy and dense as a full orchestra chord held out at a fortissimo level. Timbre is also the very first musical element that young babies (and babies *in utero*) can differentiate (McDonald & Simons, 1989).

Students should be made aware of the fine and sublime timbre possibilities of the sounds they create. Urge students to think sensitively about their timbre choices—even if it is as simple as thinking about the way they hold a mallet to strike the bar of a xylophone (there are infinite and subtle possible timbral variations in this choice). Continually asking students to think about their timbre choices will enhance their experience as musicians and composers.

In order to emphasize the importance of timbre through composition assignments, occasionally ask students to change just one sound in one of their compositions. What sound might they change, and how, in order to make a drastic difference in the effect of the composition? What sound could they substitute to make a less obvious change?

Music composition software offers a large and varied palette of timbres for students to explore and manipulate. Computer technology now puts hundreds of authentic and rich sounds at users' fingertips. One of the first assignments I give when working with students in a computer composition class is to have them spend a long period of time exploring all of the different timbres available to them, and then choose their favorite ten. This "forced" exploration gets them to listen to a wide range of sounds before settling too quickly on a favorite. With so many timbre options, such as in a program like GarageBand, giving such direction will guide students to listen more carefully and discriminately. I find that students are often pleasantly surprised when they stumble upon sounds they have never heard. This same exercise could be done with a variety of different mallets on a mallet instrument. Which ones make the most interesting timbre? What if you use a different end of the mallet to make a sound? What if the mallet strikes a different place on the bar? Introducing the world of the subtleties of timbre, and the simplicity in controlling and changing timbre, provides a wonderful "ear-opening" experience for students. This takes time and patience, and I would say should be made deliberate in almost all music composition activities.

Texture

Texture is the combining of sounds to produce an interesting "fabric." In its most basic sense, texture in music can be described as thick or thin, homophonic, monophonic, or polyphonic. The graphics in figure 6.3 are ones that I use to help illustrate these concepts.

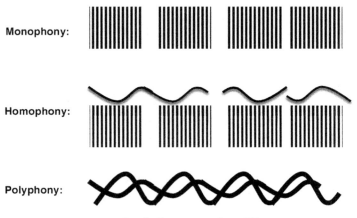

FIGURE 6.3 Iconic Representation of Textures

Fabric analogies for texture provide a rich catalyst for composition assignments (as well as have rich potential for integrated art projects). Provide samples of fabric, ranging from a white cotton sheet to coarse and patterned burlap and ask students, using whatever instruments are available, to compose music that matches the texture of one of the fabrics. Explore the meaning of thick and thin texture by listening to a variety of musical recordings—and match these to the fabrics as well.

A more "rule-bound" composition assignment intended to teach a concept within texture could revolve around composing music that is polyphonic (e.g., a simple recorder or flute duet). Pair students on bell sets (or band/orchestra instruments or voices), and ask them to compose a duet in which each part is independent from every other. The parts should wind around one another, sound independent, and also sound good together. A follow-up assignment to this would be to compose a duet in which one part is the main part and the second is more an accompaniment. Ask more advanced students to use standard notation to notate their compositions; less advanced students will simply draw a graphic representation. One "rule" for such an assignment should be that it sounds good to the composer. Students should justify why they enjoy their composition, and more advanced students might be required to use technical musical terms for this justification. As students compose aesthetically interesting compositions, they can retrospectively learn about the harmonic rules they've used to see *why* they sound the way they do.

Of course, texture, like the other elements, can be combined with any of the other elements, though texture and pitch work best together when learning about these concepts.

Density

Ethnomusicologist Bruno Nettl wrote an oft-cited essay on musical improvisation in which he attempts to articulate a method for comparing improvisations from all cultures using a universal framework (Nettl, 1974). "Density" is one of the descriptors he uses and defines it as how close together or far apart familiar "points of reference" fall in a given model. He writes:

> In comparing various types of models, we find that those of jazz are relatively dense, those of Persian music, of medium density, and those of an Arabic *taqsim* or an Indian *alap,* relatively lacking in density. Figure bass, and Baroque music in which a soloist improvises ornamentation, are perhaps the densest models of all. (Nettl, 1974, p. 13)

I think of Nettl's description as defining a horizontal density: the frequency of recurring events or familiar markers over time. We can also imagine density on a vertical level—that is how many pitches are being played simultaneously. On the horizontal axis density is related to the intensity of music and on the vertical axis, density is related to sheer force and volume (essentially, more is louder). Density combines all of the elements described above. The frequency of changes (in chords or rhythms or melodies) as well as the thinness or thickness of the texture or simultaneous events provides the feeling of density for the listener. I'm not certain that composers plan *a priori* their decisions about density in a composition, but these decisions likely come into play as they plan more globally for the overall effect or impact of a composition.

At the most basic level, students should be aware of, and make choices about, the dynamics of their music. As they compose more, then decisions about the effect of density on the affective impact of a composition should also be part of the discussion.

Conclusion

In this chapter I have offered thoughts and ideas for teaching music composition *through* the musical elements of pitch (including melody and harmony), rhythm, timbre, texture, and density. Exercises geared around the musical elements should be presented after students have explored and listened and experimented with free-form composition as suggested in the curriculum sequence model. The composition assignments that go hand in hand with teaching the musical elements tend to be more parameter driven, or rule-bound, in order to teach *about* the musical elements than those in earlier chapters. The composition activities that accompany any music lesson in which a concept is being learned are as open to possibilities as one's imagination. Having students discover a concept first, through their own aural and aesthetic manipulation via composition, will make the conceptual understanding of that concept much more meaningful and musical. Remember: What are you teaching today? Compose it!

Composition Exercises

ACTIVITY 6A: Beginner: Compose a Melody

Rationale: The concept of melody, although simple to most of us, is an interesting one to present to young children, and though one might assume that beginners understand the term, my experience shows me that this is far from true. There is no better way to decide if a learner "gets" melody than asking him or her to compose a simple one. One can explore melody in many ways, but the following lesson is one of the first that I use to have children experiment with the composition of a melody. I do not believe in restricting time signature, length, key signature, or any other parameters to begin with. This assignment works beautifully as a springboard for more "parameter-driven" melody assignments later.

Level/Type: Beginning composers of any age.

Materials:
• Any melody capable instrument (e.g., recorder or tone bells); for this lesson, a 1.5-octave simple bell set for each child
• Paper and writing tools

Objectives: Students will:
• Compose a short melody for a bell set
• Notate their original melody
• Perform their original melody

Length: One class period

Preparation: Introduce the concept of melody by pointing out melodies sung or performed in class—refer often to the definition of a melody (presented earlier). Use familiar melodies such as "Happy Birthday" or themes from TV shows as examples, and refer to the last note as the "home tone," or the note that makes the melody feel final.

Procedures: Step 1. Provide each student with a bell set (this could also work with pairs of students).

Step 2. Hand out paper and pencil for notation.

Step 3. Give out or display the following directions:
• *Use "C" as your "home note."*
• *Play around with the bells to make up a melody you like that uses the home note during the melody and ends on the home note.*
• *Memorize your melody, and give it a title. Write it down on paper (standard or graphic notation) to help you remember it.*
• *Practice your melody so you can play it for class.*

Assessment: Are students able to:

✓ Compose a melody that uses only one note in succession at a time?

✓ End their melody on C as their home note?

✓ Perform their melody more than one time the same way?

✓ Notate their melody to help them remember it?

Extensions and   • Students decide on their home tone (rather than C).

Variations: • Work in pairs, with one student (or both) coming up with words to go with the melody.

• Students use a simple poem and create a melody to go with it (either sung or on bells).

• Students exchange melodies and teach one another their melody based on their notations.

ACTIVITY 6B: Intermediate: Applause! Graphic Notation

Rationale: There are many instances when standard notation simply does not
                suffice for getting across the intention of a composer. In fact, graphic
                notation sometimes works better than the traditional. Being precise
                with graphic notation is not easy, yet preciseness is the key for
                successful communication between composer and performer. In this
                project, students will use graphic notation in order to convey musical
                meaning in a creative and exploratory way, as well as to think about
                ways in which the musical elements can be combined. Composer
                Bernard Rands composed a wonderful series of contemporary music
                for young players that utilizes graphic notation* in this manner.
                Another score, *Burst of Applause* by Vito Mason, also presents a
                model example of a graphic score with precise timing, rhythm,
                volume and tessitura effects. *Burst of Applause* is for clapping hands
                using a variety of techniques to change sounds, range, dynamics,
                and so on. These scores can serve as examples for students in this
                project.

Level/Type: Intermediate. Group or individual.

Materials: • Examples of professional scores with graphic notation
                • Score paper (9 × 14 plain paper) and pencil
                • Access to miscellaneous instruments (optional) or just use of hands/
                  body percussion

Objectives: Students will:
                • Create a composition for an ensemble of four to eight members
                  using precise graphic notation and lasting at least 30 seconds
                • Provide notation parameters for pitch, rhythm, timbre, texture, and
                  density throughout the composition

Length: One class period for introduction. At least a week for students to
                compose (either at school or as homework). Two or three class
                periods for composers to rehearse and then perform their music
                compositions.

Preparation: Familiarize students with scores such as *Sound Patterns 1* by Bernard
                Rands or *Burst of Applause* by Vito Mason or any score that uses
                graphic notation. Note the very precise information regarding pitch,
                rhythm, textures, and so on.

Procedures: Step 1. Have students decide upon an ensemble and instruments for which to write. They should choose between four and eight members and decide on the voices or instruments used based on the options and performers that are available (i.e., Who will perform? Do they feel comfortable using their voices? Should they only clap? Are there classroom instruments available?).

Step 2. Instructions: *Write a composition for four to eight performers that lasts at least 30 seconds. Explore ways to manipulate and notate pitch, rhythm, timbre, texture, and density. Provide in your score clear graphic notation to indicate performance specifications. Include directions for timing, dynamics, styles, range, and any other performance details in order to realize your composition through a performance.*

Step 3. Give student composers the opportunity to work with their ensemble members to teach them the composition and to rehearse it.

Step 4. Perform compositions in class or on a composition recital.

Assessment: Are students able to:

✓ Compose a composition for four to eight members that is at least 30 seconds long?

✓ Notate their composition using graphic notation and clearly indicating performance instructions for pitch, rhythm, timbre, texture, and density?

✓ Teach their composition to an ensemble that results in a satisfactory performance?

Extensions and Variations:
• Limit the composition to only clapping or to only words/voices.
• Compose for a full ensemble such as a band, orchestra or choir using graphic notation.

Recordings and Other Resources:
• Any music score that uses graphic notation (such as those in Bernard Rands's music for young players series).
• Mason, V. (1972). *Burst of Applause.* Bryn Mawr, PA: Theodore Presser (out of print).

*Examples of Rands's scores include *Agenda* (1970) and *Per Esempio* (1969) for youth orchestra; *Sound Patterns 1* (1967) for voices and hands; *Sound Patterns 2* (1967) for voices, percussion, and miscellaneous instruments; *Sound Patterns 3* (1969) for voices; and *Sound Patterns 4* (1969) for miscellaneous instrumental groups. All scores are under the copyright of European American Music distributors.

ACTIVITY 6C: Advanced: Adding Harmony to Melodies

Rationale:	This assignment takes the ideas presented in activity 6D and extends it to writing for a large ensemble. Here students are pushed to take ideas from a melody they write, add some harmonic components, and then arrange it for a chorus. Prerequisites would include advanced knowledge of voice ranges and advanced standard notation knowledge. This would work as a wonderful assignment for a student who has been composing and shows a real interest to advance by composing for a performing ensemble such as a choir. There are no specific guidelines to follow except to allow the student time to try out ideas throughout the process.
Level/Type:	Advanced. Individual.
Materials:	Manuscript paper or notation software
Objectives:	Students will: • Compose a simple melody with lyrics and harmony • Arrange the melody for an SATB choir
Length:	One semester (or more)
Preparation:	A student who undertakes this project should have had some basic theory as well as experience in composing.
Procedures:	Step 1. Have the student sketch a melody with lyrics and then add simple chord tones to accompany it (See activity 6D). Step 2. Write the melody for the soprano section. Step 3. Divide the chord tones into notes and passing notes for the alto, tenor, and bass sections. Step 4. If desirable, pass the melody to different sections (arrange as desired). Step 5. Write an appropriate introduction and ending.
Assessment:	Are students able to: ✓ Compose and notate music with lyrics for an SATB choir?
Extensions and Variations:	• This assignment could be extended to arranging for band or orchestra. • Students could add a piano accompaniment to a choral composition.
Recordings and Other Resources:	• Ostrander, A. E., and Wilson, D. (1986). *Contemporary Choral Arranging*. Upper Saddle River, NJ: Prentice Hall.

ACTIVITY 6D: Technology: Chord Fun

Rationale: If given a palette of chords from which to choose, how would students
                 order them in a way that sounds best to them? This is the idea of
                 "Chord Fun." Using a basic software notation program students are
                 given chord choices and then asked to put them in an order that
                 sounds good to them. They then add a melody on top of this
                 progression. After this exercise students can learn about basic chord
                 function and see how their ears led them to a dominant-tonic ending
                 (or not). The idea is for the theory to come after the aural exercise so
                 that students may manipulate the sounds before learning the rules.

Level/Type: Beginning composers of any age.

Materials: • Computer stations equipped with notation software
                 • Notation software template set up for solo with piano accompani-
                   ment and with 5 given chords.

Objectives: Students will:
                 • Arrange 5 given chords into a progression over 8 measures.
                 • Add a melody to the chords in which the first note of each measure
                   is one of the chord tones.
                 • Defend their chord progression choices.

Length: Two class periods

Preparation: Previous to this lesson students should have a basic understanding of
                 the concept of consonant "chords" (three notes at a time, every other
                 note). They should also have some familiarity with a music notation
                 software program. Prepare a notation template using a music
                 notation software program in which the staff includes a melody line
                 with piano accompaniment. Arrange 5 chords in the first 5 measures
                 of the piano accompaniment (these chords should include at least
                 the I, IV, and V chords in the key, and two other random chords),
                 followed by 8 empty measures.

Procedures: Step 1. Students work at their individual computer stations to complete
                 the following assignment for the Chord Fun template:
                 • *Copy and paste the given chords to fill out 8 measures.*
                 • *Each chord should be used at least once.*
                 • *Next add a simple melody to go with the chords in the melody staff.*
                 • *The first beat of every measure should be a chord tone. Use only
                   quarter, half, and eighth notes or rests for the melody.*

Step 2. Upon completion, have students either share aloud, or write a paragraph describing why they put the chords in the order that they did.

Assessment:

Are students able to:

✓ Use all 5 given chords at least once over 8 measures?

✓ Create a melody above the chord tones in which the first beat of every measure is one of the chord tones?

✓ Create a melody that uses only quarter, half, and eighth notes and rests?

✓ Describe their reasons for their chord progression order?

Extensions and Variations:

• Students break up the chord tones into an arpeggiated accompaniment.

• Students add a B section and then paste their beginning section to create an ABA composition.

• Students create a duet line to go with the melody.

ACTIVITY 6E: Ensemble: Melody Writing for an Instrument

Rationale: Why not have students begin writing simple melodies as soon as they begin on an instrument? As soon as students learn 3 notes, they can begin writing original melodies for their instruments. With each new note (or rhythm or time signature or key signature, etc.), have students write a new composition. Their original composition can serve as one of the exercises to be practiced in place of one or two lines in their method books. Students not only get excited about writing their *own* practice tunes, but they will practice them much more than those in a book. A sense of pride and identity as a composer will develop from this beginning stage of learning an instrument. Weekly composition exercises will also strengthen music reading skills.

Level/Type: Beginning instrumentalists of any age.

Materials:
- Wind, percussion, or string instrument
- Staff manuscript paper and pencil

Objectives: Students will:
- Compose a melody for their instrument using the notes that they know
- Perform their melody

Length: Repeated throughout a lesson year

Preparation: Students will need a basic introduction to manuscript paper. Give students an opportunity to practice writing the clef for their instrument, time signatures, and notes on the manuscript paper.

Procedures: The following instructions might accompany a melody writing exercise for beginning instrumentalist:

Step 1. *Create a simple 4-measure melody for your instrument by following these steps. Use only quarter notes and half notes.*

Step 2. *Play around on your instrument trying to find ideas for a simple melody using E♭, F, G, and B♭ (your first 4 notes!).*

Step 3. *Notate your melody on the manuscript paper provided.*

Step 4. *Practice your melody so that you can perform it.*

It is always important to include the last step whereby students can actually play what they write so they do not write anything too outlandish.

Assessment: Are students able to:
                          ✓ Notate an original melody with the given notes and rhythms?
                          ✓ Perform their melody?

Extensions and   • Students write a solo for the teacher (giving them more notes and
Variations: rhythms to choose from).

                      • Student melodies are performed by the class or ensemble on a
                        weekly basis (good sight-reading exercise).

                      • Students write melodies for one another.

ACTIVITY 6F: Sound Textures

Rationale: This lesson uses a visual to inspire composing around "thick" or "thin" density of textures. Texture and density in music is sometimes best learned through interdisciplinary lessons. Music from the minimalist composer Morton Feldman provides a wonderful example of how a composer uses a painting to inspire his music. In the case of the Mark Rothko paintings that inspired Feldman, we are provided with an almost "nontexture" example of music, which is in contrast to his music inspired by a complex pattern in a Persian rug. This lesson opens up options of exploring texture and density through patterns and feeling of cloth and rugs.

Level/Type: Beginning or intermediate composers of any age.

Materials: • Any large variety of classroom and/or nontraditional instruments
   • A variety of textiles, cloths, blankets, or rugs that each have different and varied textures and patterns

Objectives: Students will:
   • Compose minimalist music inspired by a textile
   • Describe how their musical choices mimic the texture and density of the stimulus
   • Describe their music using texture and density terms such as thick, thin, homophony, monophony and/or polyphony
   • Perform their composition

Length: One to two class periods

Preparation: Introduce the concept of *minimalism* in music by playing *Clapping Music* by Steve Reich. The layering and entrances of hand claps in this recording create a polyphony, but in a very minimalist style. Play *Crippled Symmetry* by Morton Feldman as an example of minimalist music inspired by a Turkish rug. (More history of minimalism in music and the time period could extend this lesson into several days.) Discuss the *texture* of the minimalist music (if need be, introduce the terms *monophony*, *homophony*, and *polyphony* in this description; ideally students would have learned these terms previous to this lesson.) Discuss whether the density of the music examples is either thick or thin, and how the music causes this illusion.

Procedures: Step 1. Create groups of three or four students to work together.
   Step 2. Each group decides (or is assigned) to compose music to a textile provided by the teacher.

Step 3. Groups gather appropriate instruments and begin composing their music composition. The composition should last at least 2 minutes.

Step 4. Upon completion, groups perform music for one another (if they do not know which textile inspired each others' compositions, at this point the class could guess).

Step 5. The composers write a paragraph describing the texture of their composition using words such as *thick*, *thin*, *homophony*, *polyphony*, and *monophony*. In addition, they defend their use of sounds and how the sounds relate to the textile that inspired their composition.

Assessment:

Are students able to:

✓ Create a 2-minute composition that reflects texture and density in a given textile?

✓ Describe their music using texture and density terms?

Extensions and Variations:

• Students create their own artwork or textile to inspire a composition.

• Work with the visual art teacher to venture into other artworks that might inspire minimalist type of composing, such as those by Jackson Pollock or M. C. Escher.

• Students work individually or in pairs using computer software such as GarageBand to compose their music.

Recordings and Other Resources:

• Feldman, M. (1970, 1978). Rothko Chapel 3 & Why Patterns [Recorded by the California EAR Unit]. On *Rothko Chapel* [Audio CD]. Tivoli, NY: New Albion Records (2009).

• Feldman, M. (1983). Crippled Symmetry Region A [Recorded by the California Ear Unit]. On *Crippled Symmetry (Disc 1)* [Audio CD]. New Rochelle, NY: Bridge Records (1999).

• Reich, S. (1966). Clapping Music. On *Steve Reich: Early Works* [Audio CD]. New York: Nonesuch Records (1992).

• Rothko paintings

Big Elements

The creative person is able to transform the sea of irrelevancy in which he finds himself into a vision of order and beauty, or he sees how a tiny fragment of seeming cosmic futility collides and coincides with a piece of obviousness.

SILVANO ARIETI, *Creativity*

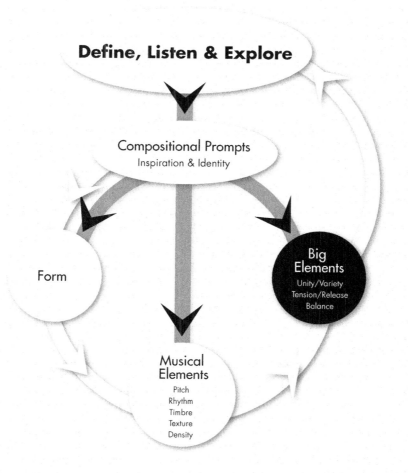

What is on your iPod right now? What are your top two favorite music selections of all times? Listen to these carefully, and try to figure out what it is that makes them favorites. What is it about great music that makes it interesting? What makes us want to listen again and again and again to our favorite selections? One can follow all sorts of guidelines to create beautifully arranged chord patterns; one can easily put a string of notes together to make a simple melody; in fact, it is not difficult at all to create a collage of random sounds from virtually any sound-making tool in our midst. But what is it that makes the very best music of our time (or the favorite music on our iPods) create such a lasting impact? Why are listeners drawn to some music and not others? What makes some music last through the ages, while others are one hit wonders? Although these questions are not easy to answer, they make for wonderful discussion prompts with children and adults who are interested in composing music. The answers to these questions should guide the composition process.

This chapter, and the final point in the five-stage curriculum model, is about that which makes music interesting. I call these the "big elements," and they are (a) unity and variety, (b) tension and release, and (c) balance. Consider the "big elements" as the key to composing music that makes it more than just an exercise in combining pitches. Before delving into the specific thoughts about these three areas, I begin this chapter by examining what makes music good, overall, and how we might bring this discussion into our classrooms in order to make students not only more conscientious and broad consumers of music, but also better composers. Then I discuss more specific ideas for getting students to think about the three big elements in classroom composition projects.

What Makes Music "Good"?

Sociologists, cognitive psychologists, and behavioral psychologists might offer different answers to the question of how music moves us. Certainly the social circumstance and rituals and ceremonies and rules of listening all play into the overall impact of music, as Christopher Small so eloquently reminds readers in *Musicking* (1998).

Music is so very powerful, and often in the rush to "teach" it, we sometimes forget to simply enjoy its overall effect. How is it that the music is so powerful as to tug at hearts and souls? And how can teachers make this point in music classrooms? It is this section of the composition curriculum that highlights the big elements—the elements that make music interesting. The concepts of unity and variety, tension and release, and balance are useful tools to make compositions more interesting than ordinary.

Aesthetician and psychologist Leonard Meyer spent a lifetime exploring this very question of how it is that music moves us, and offers a theory that I use with students when approaching the question at this point in the curriculum. His landmark text, *Emotion and Meaning in Music* (1961) is a remarkable tome that works to answer many of the questions posed above. When having a discussion about "good music" with students, I break down Meyer's theory into the following (albeit extremely simplified) four points:

1. Listeners know one (and occasionally more) syntactical style of music. They can sense the patterns inherent in a familiar style.
2. Listeners have expectations about music. For instance, in Western tonal music they expect pitches and rhythms to provide interest and variety yet sound cohesive and unified, often centered around a tonal center.
3. Composers usually write music that follows the expected musical patterns. An expectancy is set up, and then a tendency is fulfilled.
4. Emotion or affect is aroused when a tendency is arrested or inhibited. Composers play with the speed with which tendencies are fulfilled.

Tension and release, unity and variety, and balance are those elements that play with the expectation and release that listeners experience in music. Using these big elements as a starting point can aid students in thinking about composing music that affects their listeners.

An Activity

I often begin this unit by focusing on the great melodies of all times. We brainstorm a list of melodies that students know and remember. Invariably the list includes such great tunes as "Amazing Grace" and "Over the Rainbow," as well as something from the latest top hit (which I likely do not know). I offer up the very simple melody from the Largo movement of Dvorak's Symphony No. 9 in E Minor as well as some old TV theme songs that the entire class may be familiar with as examples of effective melodies. With older students I plunk some of these out on the piano and we listen and analyze the structure: What note do they start and end on? How wide is the overall interval span? Are there repeated notes? What kinds of steps, leaps, contour? Are there any patterns common among all of them? With younger students I provide a handout with the notation of some very simple and common melodies such as "Frère Jacques," "Twinkle Twinkle Little Star," and "Happy Birthday." The next step is to divide the students into small groups with the assignment that they come up with a list of four "rules" that apply to all good melodies (or at least the ones we deem as good in the discussion leading up to this). In other words, what rules are common among melodies that, if we were to follow, would allow us to compose our own good and memorable melodies?

The remarkable outcome to this exercise is that students will invariably come up with four rules that are not only similar among themselves, but also contain some of the same features from Meyer's principles (listed above). Some common discoveries include the following: the clever avoidance of tonic to set up expectation for a resolution, a balance between steps and leaps and repeated notes, a balanced contour, and often a downward motion at the end.

We continue this exercise by unpacking music that is harmonically and rhythmically interesting as well. How do chords move? What are the commonalities? What rhythms work well in a certain selection? Why? By doing this, it is easy to see Meyer's principles come alive before our ears and eyes. It is after these discovery exercises that I share Meyer's principles with students and we begin to delve into ways in which we could do this in music. We then play with the ideas of unity and variety, tension and release, and balance in music. These big elements help bring awareness to how music affects the listener.

The big elements in music are also quite evident in other arts areas. In fact they lend themselves to very rich possibilities for integrated arts lessons and coteaching with related arts teachers. In the paragraphs that follow, I offer some brief thoughts about each of these big elements and include ideas for combining lessons with other arts areas.

Unity and Variety

"Same and different" is one of the early concepts we teach children, not only in music class, but also in most other subjects. The fundamental concept of same and different fits with Meyer's points 1 and 2 above: all listeners are familiar with at least one style of music, yet need variety in this style to stay interested. This also follows the principles outlined in music preference literature (e.g., Hargreaves, 1984; Miller, 1992). That is, if listeners hear something they are not familiar with, they may not like it at first, but repeated listenings will raise their preference level. The more that a listener becomes familiar with complex music, the more likely he or she is likely to enjoy it. However, too much of the same thing also works against us: listeners become bored and lose interest in music that is too much the same or has been listened to too often. The balance between sameness and difference is a remarkable, yet relatively simple, tool that composers can use to affect listeners.

In music, ideas related to "unity and variety" can lead to many composing and improvising activities, as well as moments for teaching same and different. Theme and variation is the most obvious form that exemplifies unity and variety. Any theme that students are working with, be it in the band class or in a general music text, can easily be composed into variations. An example of a simple improvisation exercise is to sit students in a circle and have a lead student improvise a short theme. Each student around the circle then improvises a variation to the theme. This can be done with similar instruments (e.g., all barred xylophones) or very different instruments (a random variety of barred instruments and percussive instruments) or even voices. It is a great activity not only for improvising while learning about unity and variety, but also for ear training.

Unity and variety are concepts that are apparent in visual art and therefore work well for integrated lessons with visual art and music. Visual artists work to achieve the same/different balance just as musical composers do. There are many rich lesson possibilities that could come out of pairing visual art and music around this theme of unity and variety.

Tension and Release

One of my favorite moments in music that illustrates a composer playing with tension and release in music comes at the end of the Largo section of Dvorak's Symphony No. 9 in E Minor. The beautiful melody comes back at the end of this movement after a middle section of very different and animated musical themes. When the melody finally comes back, played by an English horn solo, Dvorak "teases" the listener by introducing the beginning of the melody, but interrupts it with a long pause. And finally it finishes with a satisfying conclusion. There are many similar examples in music that teachers and students can find and analyze whereby they sense the buildup of tension and then a release by the composer. Dissonance, consonance, repetition, pauses, and changes are all tools that composers use to play with the emotional tension and release that affect listeners.

Related areas that work well to illustrate the concept of tension and release are literature and movies. What is it, exactly, in a movie, or story, that causes tension buildup? What is it about a story that makes it difficult to put a book down or makes one desperate to turn the page? In movies, it is often the underlying soundtrack that contributes to feelings of tension. The brilliance of any composer, movie writer, or author is in his or her ability to perfectly balance the tension and let the listener (or reader or observer) feel this release at just the right moment. Use improvisation activities to illustrate tension and release. Have one group of students build up a tension with instruments or voices and another to resolve the tension that was built. Doing it and feeling it through improvised activities are ways to illustrate the feelings and may help students to purposefully and skillfully utilize tension and release methods in their compositions.

Balance

When I first bring up the idea of balance to students, they think I mean stereo balance, that is, just the right amount of bass and treble, or left-to-right speaker proportions. Balance is probably the most abstract idea to teach, but the simplest to feel and understand. Balance happens when there is just the right amount of unity and variety, or tension and release, to make the listener appreciate the music. A balanced musical moment keeps the listener coming back for more. One way to begin with this concept is to play a variety of four or five successful musical compositions. Ask students to listen and write down their thoughts about why the music feels balanced to them (or why it does not). Share and discuss the answers in order to bring the class to a clarification about balance in effective music. As in Meyer's fourth principle from above, in a well-balanced composition, the composer fulfills a tendency with just the right amount of speed.

What is balance in artwork? It happens when we look at a painting and feel that the right amount of color or shapes are spread strategically and artfully across the canvas. Working with visual art or architecture can help to make this concept clear, but it is one that will take time in the classroom to make sense. Visit it, discuss it, compose balanced and unbalanced music, and keep coming back to it to encourage students to continually think about balance in their own compositions.

What makes music interesting? This is the basic question when thinking about composing or improvising. Keep this question in mind when having students compose. Ask them, and discuss why they like the music they like in terms of the big elements of unity and balance, tension and release, and balance. These are the tools we can use to encourage students to begin composing music that is interesting.

Composition Exercises

ACTIVITY 7A: Beginner: Theme and Variation

Rationale: Introduce the idea of unity and variety in music through the concept
                    of theme and variation. Although music might include some that is
                    same, and some that is different, the parts sound like they belong
                    together. How might we compose same/different in a manner that
                    sound like they belong together?

Level/Type: Beginning composers in an elementary music classroom.

Materials: A variety of barred and percussive classroom instruments

Objectives: Students will:
                    • Compose 15-second sections of music as a variety (different) to a
                      given theme
                    • Notate their compositions using nontraditional notation

Length: Two class sessions: one class for group work and one for performances

Preparation: Begin by reviewing the concept of *same* and *different* in music by
                    going over previous lessons when these concepts were taught. Play
                    renditions of music that are the "same" but different: for example,
                    the very many different renditions of the "The Star Spangled Banner"
                    is one clear example. Note that the composer makes the music sound
                    as if belongs together even when the theme is changed.

Procedures: Step 1. Have children sit in a circle holding a variety of musical
                    instruments. The teacher plays from her instrument a short theme
                    (6–8 notes). Each person around the circle is then to follow with
                    something different, but sounding like it belongs. Continue this
                    around the circle until the end.
                    Step 2. Divide students into groups of three to four. In their groups,
                    students are to compose a composition that follows a "same/
                    different/same" form. They are to first create a "theme" that they
                    play together as a group. Then they compose a "different" section
                    that sounds different yet still belongs. They finish their composition
                    with the theme.
                    Step 3. Have students illustrate, in nontraditional notation, their
                    composition using markers on large paper. The notation will be a
                    visual reinforcement of the same/different/same form.
                    Step 4. Each group performs their composition for the class.

Assessment: Are students able to:

✓ Compose a composition with 3 sections (same/different/same) that sound like they belong together?

✓ Draw nontraditional notation to illustrate their musical composition form?

Extensions and Variations:

• Have all of the students use the same theme and compose different sections. Compare to see which sound the most cohesive with the theme. String together a number of different sections to create a longer composition.

ACTIVITY 7B: Intermediate: Perform My Artwork

Rationale: A method to help students begin to understand the abstract ideas of
                  unity/variety, tension/release, and balance is to have them attempt
                  to create visual representations of these ideas first. The following
                  exercise can be modified in several ways for any number of different
                  classroom configurations. It is a fun exercise and can also help to
                  point to the potential for connection between what we visualize and
                  what we hear through music.

Level/Type: Any.

Materials: • A variety of musical instruments (classroom instruments or band/
                    orchestra instruments)
                  • Large (poster-size) paper
                  • A variety of colored markers or crayons

Objectives: Students will:
                  • Create a visual representation of unity/variety, tension/release, or
                    balance
                  • Interpret a visual representation (drawn by other students) of unity/
                    variety, tension/release, or balance by using it as a musical score to
                    create and perform an original musical composition

Length: One to two class sessions (depending on the time of a class, one
                  period may be taken for the visual part of this exercise and the
                  second period for the performance)

Preparation: Precede this exercise with an introduction to the concept of unity/
                  variety, tension/release, and balance. Discuss the concepts in class,
                  and listen to musical examples that help to illustrate these terms.

Procedures: Step 1. Divide the students into groups of three or four. Hand each
                  group a large piece of paper with either U/V (unity/variety), T/R
                  (tension/release), or B (balance) written in pencil in small print in the
                  corner. After each group is aware of their designated element, have
                  them erase the letters and not let the other groups know what they
                  have.
                  Step 2. Students work in their groups to create a visual representation
                  of their assigned element. They should discuss and plan first and
                  sketch out ideas on scrap paper before creating their poster-size
                  rendition. Their visual representation has no parameters: it is what
                  comes to their minds when they think of the big elements they are
                  given.

Step 3. After the groups are finished with their drawings, collect them and randomly redistribute them to other groups. The groups are now to use the drawing as a musical score. They should work together to choose musical instruments (if classroom instruments) and to compose a musical composition that uses the pictures as their "score" inspiration.

Step 4. Each group performs their composition for the class, with the "score" (visual representation) posted so all can see. At this point students in the class (as well as the group of performers) try to guess which of the three elements the visual scores was trying to represent: unity/variety, tension/release, or balance. Respondents should defend their choices to lead to a discussion of why they believe what might be represented.

Step 5. The original "artists" of the drawing will reveal the element they drew and describe their choices for their drawing.

Assessment:

Are students able to:

✓ Visually illustrate one of the three "big idea" (unity/variety, tension/release, balance) elements?

✓ Create a musical composition inspired by a graphic "score"?

✓ Discuss and defend reasons for seeing or hearing unity/variety, tension/release, or balance in a score or original composition?

Extensions and Variations:

• Begin by first having a group of students compose a musical composition that depicts one of the three elements (unity/variety, tension/release, or balance), and then ask another group of students to create the visual depiction of the music, still trying to guess what the designation is.

• Work with the visual arts teacher to compose music and corresponding visual representations of the three big elements of unity/variety, tension/release, and balance.

• Compose music that contains *only* tension, or *only* variety, or *no* balance.

ACTIVITY 7C: Advanced: More with Less: Minimalism

Rationale:	What happens when a composer uses as little material as possible? This question, and the ensuing exercise to compose in a minimalist manner, forces students to be economical in their choices yet think of ways they can use unity/variety, tension/release, and balance in their compositions. Minimalist composers of the twentieth century provide great examples of constraint and patience in building tension and then release in their music.
Level/Type:	Secondary school students or students with previous composing experience.
Materials:	• Any instrument • Paper and writing tool
Objectives:	Students will: • Compose a minimalist-style composition for either an ensemble or solo piano • Notate their composition so that others can perform it
Length:	One week
Preparation:	Learn about the history of minimalist composers, such as Steve Reich, Philip Glass, Morton Feldman, and Terry Riley, and listen to their music. Here are some recommended listening pieces: • Movement I "Sosenuto—Misurato—Prestissimo" of György Ligeti's *Musica Ricercata* (in this movement Ligeti uses only one pitch—D—in multiple ways until ending on the last note of A) • "Crippled Symmetry Region A," by Morton Feldman • *Two Pages*, by Philip Glass • *Music for 18 Musicians*, by Steve Reich • *In C*, by Terry Riley
Procedures:	Step 1. Students should be familiar with concepts and techniques of minimalist composers. Have them choose one of the following to create their music composition: • Work with 3 pitches in a composition that lasts at least 3 minutes. Make changes gradually (imperceptibly, if possible) over time. OR • Use 4 different chords in a composition that lasts at least 3 minutes. Make changes gradually (imperceptibly, if possible) over time. Step 2. Notate the composition for an appropriate performer (either piano or an ensemble).

Assessment: Are students able to:
  ✓ Compose music using a limited pitch set in a minimalist style?
  ✓ Notate their composition for an accurate performance?

Extensions and Variations:
• Ideas for extending minimalist composing are endless—variable by ensemble or choice of timbre or limited rhythms.

Recordings and Other Resources:
• Feldman, M. (1983). Crippled Symmetry Region A [Recorded by the California Ear Unit]. On *Crippled Symmetry* (Disc 1) [Audio CD]. New Rochelle, NY: Bridge Records (1999).
• Glass, P. (1969). Two pages. On *Glass: Two Pages; Contrary Motion; Music in Fifths; Music in Similar Motion* [Audio CD]. New York: Nonesuch Records (1994).
• Ligeti, G. (1953). Musica ricercata No. 1: Sosenuto—Misurato—Prestissimo [Recorded by Pierre-Laurent Aimard]. On *Ligeti: Études, musica ricercata* [Audio CD]. New York: Sony Classical (1997).
• Reich, S. (1976). *Music for 18 Musicians* [Audio CD]. New York: Nonesuch Records (1998).
• Riley, T. (1964). In C [Recorded by Margaret Hassell]. On *Terry Riley in C* [Audio CD]. New York: Sony Classics (2009).

ACTIVITY 7D: Technology: Ostinato

Rationale: The following exercise, built around the concept of an ostinato pattern, helps to illustrate all three of the big elements of unity/variety, tension/release, and balance. It works well using a computer sequencing program, but could easily be adapted for classroom instrument use.

Level/Type: Upper level elementary or older.

Materials:
- Computer with music sequencing software connected to a MIDI keyboard
- Headphones

Objectives: Students will:
- Compose music utilizing an ostinato pattern following given specifications

Length: One class session

Preparation: Provide the template in figure 7.1 for students to follow in layering their ostinato composition.

Procedure: Provide the following instructions: *Create a musical composition with an ostinato accompaniment as the unifying device. Your composition should follow the form illustrated below for your musical tracks:*
- *Consider creating your ostinato as the base of your composition first, followed by the other sections.*
- *Carefully choose the track timbres to complement the others and work together as a cohesive composition.*

Assessment: Are students able to:
- ✓ Compose an ostinato composition using the form outlined above?

Extensions and Variations:
- Create a class folder of rhythmic ostinatos. Have students choose one another's ostinatos as a basis for their compositions.
- Create a multimovement composition by piecing together several different ostinato sections composed in the form described in the above lesson.

Track:	TRACK	Beginning	Middle	End
1	1	Ostinato soft & growing	Ostinato continues through this section growing gradually to a forte dynamic level. (use the paste or looping feature of the software)	Ostinato softly fades away.
2	2		Add any musical material to build variety on top of the ostinato and interest (i.e. melodies, accompaniments, tone clusters, chords)	Brief Surprise!
3	3			
4	4			
10 (perc.)	5		Optional ostinato or other rhythmic patterns added for variety or interest	

FIGURE 7.1 **Ostinato Template**

ACTIVITY 7E: Ensemble: Aleatoric Music

Rationale:	There is a growing repertoire of new music and music that includes aleatoric (improvisatory) devices for large group ensembles (i.e., band, orchestra, or choir). This kind of music is ideal for introducing the music composition and improvisation in a large ensemble class. Though the following assignment pertains to a specific piece for concert band, it can easily be adapted to any ensemble, providing that the music contains some aleatoric writing. *Epinicion* contains a simple, yet haunting, melody that repeats several times with a new background of aleatoric sounds coming from the ensemble upon each repetition. (See figure 6.1 for the melody).
Level/Type:	Intermediate- or advanced-level concert band broken into four student work groups.
Materials:	• *Epinicion* by John Paulson (Neil A. Kjos Music) • Score paper, manuscript paper, and pencils
Objectives:	Students will: • Compose a section background to the theme in *Epinicion* using aleatoric techniques • Notate their compositions for individual ensemble parts
Length:	One marking period
Preparation:	Describe the background of *Epinicion* for the students: "An epinicion is an ancient song of victory the Greeks would sing as they walked through the battlefield sorting the wounded from the dead" (excerpted from the music score). The music was written toward the end of the Vietnam War and expresses Paulson's bitterness toward the war. He uses one haunting theme to represent the chant and the aleatoric sounds for the sounds of the battlefield. Discuss with the ensemble how the use of aleatoric music is appropriate and effective for developing the mood of the piece. The calm and eerie melody represents the "release," whereas the aleatoric sounds that build provide tension. The ending of the music also provides a wonderful example of release.
Procedures:	Step 1. Divide the band into groups of four or five students. Give each group copies of a section of the score that covers one iteration of the theme. (There are eight iterations.)

Step 2. Each group should re-compose the background to their section using the following guidelines: Work as a group to compose a new background to the theme in this section by re-creating the mood and scoring using different winds and/or different effects. That is, if it has a thin texture and is soft, then keep a thin texture and soft dynamics but compose new techniques and for different instruments if you want. Do not write for instruments that are playing the theme. One group member should notate the entire section on score paper and include instructions, if needed, for band members to read. Other group members should notate the individual parts and include needed instructions on the manuscript paper provided.

Step 3. Hand out the newly composed section parts and perform *Epinicion* with the new background sections composed by groups. Discuss the effects of each of the new background section and how they are different or the same as Paulson's.

Optional: vote for the best sections for each theme iteration to perform on a concert.

Assessment: Are students able to:
✓ Compose effective (similar texture and style to those in the composition) aleatoric parts for background sections to the theme in *Epinicion*?
✓ Adequately notate and include instructions for their music in order for ensemble sections to read and perform?

Extensions and Variations: Paulson uses mostly tritones and half steps to formulate this melody. The melody is repeated several times throughout the piece—each time with a different timbre (section of the band). Have students write a melody using only 2 or 3 intervals. Choose one for the band to play, and add background aleatoric sections, effectively rewriting *Epinicion* using the same techniques as the composer, John Paulson.

Recordings and Other Resources: Aleatoric music for instrumental ensembles:
• Adler, S. (1978). *A Little Bit of . . . Space . . . Time for String Orchestra* (Grade 3). Boca Raton, FL: Ludwig Music.
• Broege, T. (1980). *Streets and Inroads: Fantasy for Winds and Percussion* (Grade 2). Brooklyn, NY: Manhattan Beach Music.
• Bukvich, D. (1986) *Dinosaurs* (Grade 3). Oshkosh, WI: Phoebus.
• Duffy, T. C. (1990). *Snakes* (Grade 2). Boca Raton, FL: Ludwig Music.
• Hodkinson, S. (1972). *A Contemporary Primer for Band* (Vols. 1 & 2). King of Prussia, PA: Theodore Presser.

- Mahr, T. (1992). *Daydream* (Grade 3). San Diego, CA: Neil A. Kjos Music.
- Oliveros, P. (1997). *Four Meditations for Orchestra* (Grade 4). Kingston, NY: Deep Listening Institute
- Paulson, J. (1975). *Epinicion* (Grade 5). San Diego, CA: Neil A. Kjos Music.
- Sweeney, M. (1994). *Ancient Voices* (Grade 1). Milwaukee, WI: Hal Leonard.

ACTIVITY 7F: Movie Soundtrack

Rationale: Much of our students' experiences with music contain a visual component. With the advent of MTV in the 1980s all the way to the current proliferation of do-it-yourself YouTube videos, a great deal of popular music today is experienced with a visual accompaniment. Music also plays a crucial role in movies. It certainly adds interest, and its absence can add tension. Including a soundtrack to a movie, by adding and then manipulating the "big elements" of sound in a movie track, is a great way for students to think about altering the overall experience of sound and visuals.

Level/Type: Intermediate/advanced.

Materials: • Computer and software (e.g., GarageBand or QuickTime) to edit movies and sound.

Objectives: Students will:
• Add music to a short video clip in two different ways: one to create tension, and the other to create humor

Length: One week

Preparation: Students should have knowledge of the software they will use to add music to a video clip. Either the teacher can prepare several premade short (30 seconds or less) and innocuous video clips or students can come up with their own. The video clips should be neutral enough so that the addition of music infuses a more obvious feeling to the video. Video clips of walking down a hallway at school, driving down the road, or an animal running about are examples of the type of video that would work best.

Procedures: Step 1. View and discuss several examples of video clips in which music plays a crucial role in setting the mood or feeling. There are countless examples available from YouTube(http://www.youtube. com). Ask: *How is it that the music composer utilizes tension and release, unity and variety, or balance to create the effect in the video?*

Step 2. Provide students with a premade 30-second (or less) video clip (or have them provide their own) and give the following instructions:

• *Compose and add music to this video clip that makes it build a feeling of tension and fright. Save it as "Fright Video."*

• *Compose and add music to the same video clip that creates a feeling of humor to the visual. Save it as "Humor Video."*

Step 3. Have students play their video clips for the class, and have classmates guess which clip (fright or humor) is being played. Discuss the compositional and musical devices used to evoke the emotion.

Assessment: Are students able to:
  ✓ Compose music for, and add music to, a video clip in order to build tension in the video clip?
  ✓ Compose music for, and add music to, a video clip in order to create humor in the video clip?

Extensions and   • Students film an "advertisement" for a product, and then add music
Variations: to the clip to sell the product.
                  • Students create music for a portion of a pre-existing movie scene. Compare their music to the original music in the scene.
                  • Students create music using classroom instruments to accompany a video clip.

Composition at the Core of School Music

Music is, for young children, primarily the discovery of sound.
G. MOORHEAD AND D. POND, *Music for Young Children*

In his book *Love, Justice, and Education: John Dewey and the Utopians*, William Schubert (2009) riffs on a little-known article by John Dewey (2006/1933)[1] that envisions what schools would be like in an imaginary, "Utopian" land. Dewey's utopian vision holds promise that "the teaching-learning environments that would bring greatest growth are not schools as we know them" (Schubert, 2009, p. 82), and both Schubert, in his contemporary take on Dewey's article, and Dewey himself imagine schools from this "Utopian" viewpoint—one in which the reader must think beyond the constraints and everyday logistics that seem to burden today's schools.

It is with the spirit of imagining what music education might be like in a Utopia that I begin this chapter. It is not a variation on Dewey's particular ideas per se (though I'm certain the idea of a composition-focused curriculum would fit nicely into Dewey's Utopian school), but my own thoughts on an ideal, utopian, music curriculum, in which composition and improvisation form the core of all music teaching and learning. In this imagined "Music Utopia Elementary School" (MUES), the main repertoire to be learned and performed is created by the children. This repertoire leads to performance, and informs listening and analysis, and naturally connects to music already written (what some might call the *classics*). In MUES, creative music making is at the center from which all other music making and learning radiate.

After describing some learning vignettes in MUES, I offer ideas about organizing a curriculum infused with composition and improvisation activities. I conclude the chapter with some final thoughts about why it is imperative that we focus our music teaching on composition and improvisation, rather than simply view these as add-on activities as they exist now.

Music Utopia Elementary School

Imagine creativity at the core rather than the periphery of music education. The focus on the end, the concert, does not need to suffer, but is likely to flourish, and the process for getting there will be more creative, intrinsically motivating, and richer than one could possibly imagine. The scenarios that follow provide glimpses into classrooms where examples of composition and improvisations are taking place. They are little snapshots in time, but hopefully offer ideas for how a teacher might teach music with creative music making at the center. The ideas for these activities come from a mixture of my experiences either observing exceptional music teachers composing and improvising with children in classrooms, or projects that I have tried myself.

MUES could be anywhere really. The size of the school or the makeup of children in the classrooms does not matter so much as the energy and dedication to creative music teaching embodied by the music teacher. The music teacher at MUES, Mr. Grainger, is in his mid-40s and entering his fifth year of teaching at MUES, with complete confidence in this approach and curriculum. He had experimented with his creative music ideas for years previous to joining the MUES faculty, and had a repetition for doing so. For this reason he was hired at MUES, because the administrators were hoping to infuse more creative activities throughout their school curriculum—and especially in the arts. Creativity matters as much as the so-called basic skills to the teachers and administrators of MUES, and they see that the music and art classes, above all other classes, are the places where students' motivation toward learning and creative thinking can flourish. The administrators at MUES realize that creativity in the arts provides a healthy balance to the sometimes stressful testing in subjects such as math and reading.

Most of Mr. Grainger's music classes begin with 3 minutes of "free play" as children enter the room. They know the routine and the rules (no louder than *mf* on any instrument, and listen first before joining in) as they improvise on a variety of instruments that often morphs into an organized "jam session." Sometimes Mr. Grainger provides a focus for the improvisation session with a word on the board or a visual cue projected on the wall. Once the improvisation comes to a natural end, Mr. Grainger launches into the lesson topic of the day.

The following "musical montages" take you into each grade classroom for a brief glimpse of music lessons at MUES. The lessons come from various points in the conceptual curriculum model introduced earlier in this book.

First Grade: Musical Elements—Texture

Mr. Grainger's room is full of colorful images and patterns. For his first-grade students, he hangs posters of black-and-white M. C. Escher images, colored Mondrian square patterns, cloths of various thickness and intricate patterns, as well as computer-generated tessellations that were created by students in the fifth grade. The students have been learning about patterns and texture in visual art as well as math, and in this particular music lesson Mr.

Grainger hopes to inspire a music composition that will reflect their understanding thus far about patterns in all areas of life.

The students are directed in their opening jam session to improvise on Escher's *Woodcut II, Strip 3*, which is hanging in the front of the room. An interesting and overlapping steady rhythmic pattern emerges, established by some children playing hand drums. Children on mallet instruments join the rhythm by improvising in a seemingly random cacophony of sounds. The music slowly fades and ends, and the children sit quietly as Mr. Grainger speaks softly: "Ooooh, I noticed the way your music faded away to a peaceful end." He points to Escher's *Woodcut II, Strip 3*, and asks "So, what do you think of this drawing?" Discussion ensues about the different kinds of birds in the image (some with eyes, some without, some with a pattern behind them). "Those of you with mallet instruments go into the corner and create a pattern that represents the left side of the image, those with hand drums, create a pattern for the middle part of the image, and those with rhythm sticks, create a pattern for the right-hand side of the image."

As the children begin to work, Mr. Grainger walks around, briefly and gently reminding the students that a pattern is a short musical idea that repeats. With 10 minutes left in class, he gathers the children back to the center of the room and asks them to share their patterns. "Now, just as Mr. Escher's print has different patterns but is one picture, how can we put these sound patterns together to make them sound like one music composition?." He skillfully directs the questions and answers from the students. "I notice that your group was playing a fast pattern, and the middle group was quite slow pattern. Who is willing to adjust to make them fit together?" Hands fly in the air, as do suggestions for change. In the end, the children compromise and Mr. Grainger conducts a quick composition made up three sections: one for each section of the drawing. He records it and dismisses the children with the promise that they will hear it again. (Many of the recordings that Mr. Grainger makes in his class get uploaded to his website for parents and students to hear, and some are played over the loudspeaker for hallway movement or to introduce the announcements for the day.) He will likely give this recording to the visual arts and math teachers who are also teaching about patterns. The art teacher may be inspired to create artwork for a CD cover.

For 5 weeks the children will delve into concepts of repeated patterns and concepts of texture in music. As they create interesting patterns on various instruments, they draw notations on index cards to help them remember, and they drop these into a "pattern box" placed at the front of the room. At times they will pull out various patterns and experiment with layering them together, either horizontally or vertically, or both, and experiment with thick and thin textures while also recalling the patterns. The children will also begin to listen for patterns in the beats of rap music, as well as in classical music (two of Mr. Grainger's favorites for these lessons are Gustav Holst's "Mars" movement from *The Planets* and Steve Reich's *Clapping Music*). In the meantime, the art students are learning about pattern (repetition, lines, shapes, colors) and texture (smooth, rough, bright, dull) in their art classes.

After the 5-week unit, all of the first-grade students will perform a concert of their "Pattern Music" while the art students display patterns and textures on the walls for a monthly MUES assembly.

Second Grade: Musical Elements—Melody

"Good morning, good morning! (sol-mi-do, sol-mi-do)" Mr. Grainger sings in a sweet falsetto as the children settle in after their free improvisation time. They respond automatically replicating his melodic "Good morning, good morning!" "Watchya doin' today Molly (do-re-mi-sol-mi-sol)?" After just a tiny hesitation Molly sings back, "Riding my bike after school, yay-a-yay," and the class kindly giggles at her improvisation. Molly continues the game as the children gather into their circle on the music rug, singing to Jack: "Watcha doin' today Jack?" Hands begin to rise, hoping that Jack will sing his response and call on them. Jack sing/raps "Going to the market gonna get me a game yo yo yo yo." And they continue around the circle until everybody has a chance to improvise a little melody. Some sing, some chant, and some rap. The students are deep into their unit on melody, learning that it is what we label any short series of notes that sound like they belong together. The challenge is to improvise a melody with their voice and also to keep track of melodies they improvise—specifically remembering the ones they really like. Mr. Grainger asks them to make notes or notations on the melodies they like in a music composition notebook.

Today the goal is to make up a catchy melody with accompaniment to a selection of silly poems from the book *Fun Limericks for Children* by Debbie Gorton. Mr. Grainger will limit their melody to do-re-mi-sol notes that he has set up on bell sets that are scattered around the room. Students will use the bell sets to aid in the creation of their melodies and will work in pairs to do so. They have been working on using these particular solfège patterns and pitch matching since the beginning of the year, and this exercise will give Mr. Grainger a chance to assess not only their singing skills but their conceptual understanding of melody as well.

The children break into pairs—each with a different limerick from the book and a bell set. Mr. Grainger provides the following simple instructions on a check-off sheet:

☐ Work with your partner to sing the limerick.
☐ Use do-re-mi-sol pitches.
☐ Use your bell set to help you.
☐ Memorize your melody and lyric.
☐ Write it down to help you remember.

At the end of class, they come back and perform for each other. Mr. Grainger records all of their melodies on his computer and later files them into their digital "process-folios." For students who will stay at the elementary school for the entire 5 years, this provides a record of their growth over time. He also uses the files often at parent visitation days to show parents what the children are composing and how they are progressing.

The following week, children will begin combining limericks and also substituting some of their own words. Some will be in charge of accompaniment parts, using Boomwhackers and hand drums. The ultimate goal is to create a "class song" that will be composed of at least three verses and chorus. Ms. Peterson, a second-grade classroom teacher, is working with rhyming in her classes and will integrate the lessons by working on rhyming with the lyrics during her teaching time. The students will compose the melody as a group and then slowly shape it into a song that describes their class. As they develop their class song, Mr. Grainger skillfully weaves in concepts from lessons on repetition, rhythm, and even harmony. This is a yearlong project, and every year second-grade students look forward to composing their class song. They bring it back (often refined) to perform at their fifth-grade graduation concert.

Third Grade: Form and Timbre

The start of today's class is filled with an amazing variety of sounds as twenty third-grade students are scurrying about the room trying different instruments to find the perfect sound. Today they are beginning the process of organizing sounds for the annual third-grade show they are writing with their classroom teacher, Mrs. Johnson. The story, which they created, is about a small child who gets lost on the way home from school and stumbles into a magical kingdom where children are in charge and adults must listen to them. It is a very funny story, and the children love it.

In art class they will create the colorful scenery and paintings that provide the visual background. In music class on this day, they are beginning to create the sounds to go with the story. "What about this for the door opening, Mr. Grainger?" Sarah asks as she sweeps her hands through a wind chime. "Remember to work this out with your teammates, Sarah. But my honest opinion? I think it's pretty cool," Mr. Grainger responds. Sarah brings her idea over to teammates Josh and Nathan, and they continue working on finding the perfect magical door sound. Their team is in charge of the introduction and beginning scene. Mr. Grainger has arranged teams of three and four students to be in charge of different sections of the story. He is using this opportunity to teach about form and timbre in music. After plotting the sound effects for each scene, students will begin to shape them into a form that makes sense for the particular scene. They will make decisions about, repetition, beginnings and endings, as well as dynamics. They will also have to carefully notate the timing for these musical backgrounds to integrate them with the text of the play.

The sounds coming from the music room are cacophonous and, some might say, noisy. Yet the students are intensely focused in their teams with clear goals as they prepare for the upcoming show. At MUES the teachers do not purchase or reuse a prepackaged musical for their annual production; rather, they work together to create something original and integrate the lessons in all of the classes to teach about the concepts they are learning.

Fourth Grade: Form and Timbre

It is spring of the fourth-grade year, and the children are learning about the food chain and food web in their science units. Mr. Grainger has cleverly thought of a way to integrate music composition into the science lessons that will help the students understand concepts associated with the food chain. During these weeks, he posts colorful images of plants and animals as well as words like *autotrophs* and *heterotrophs* around the room. Words such as *wooden, metallic, dark, bright, sharp, dull, hollow, thumpy, scratchy,* and *papery* also hang on the wall in different colors, sizes, and shapes as reminders for the students to consider different timbres when composing. Mr. Grainger uses this unit as a time to teach timbre, theme and variation, and development. Students are prompted often to think about how sounds would or would not match up with the musical ideas they are composing. The students have worked to match timbre types to various plant and animal types and have spent several lessons exploring ways to create the "sound" of a plant or animal. This project also requires the students to write using rich adjectives to describe their musical ideas.

"All right, class," Mr. Grainger says while clapping to get students' attention from around the room. "What have you decided? Will it be food chain or food web?" They had been discussing various possibilities for theme, variation, and development, and listening to examples of both. The *Variations on a Theme by Rossini* by Chopin was of particular interest because Chopin used another composer's theme. This prompted Mr. Grainger to also play Brahms's *Variations on a Theme by Haydn for Piano.* "Even back then," Mr. Grainger chuckled, "composers did covers of others' music. If other composers recreate a theme, then are they moving the music along the food chain?"

"Half of us are going to compose food web music, and the other half will compose food chain music," announces Betsy. Her classmates nod in agreement. "Don't forget to use the food web picture as your musical score," Mr. Grainger reminds them. They break into groups and begin their work: looking over the "score" and then selecting instruments with timbres that seem to work for them.

Mr. Grainger is anxious to have them perform their music in science class. He will assess their connections to the scores as well as their understanding of development and/or theme and variation that the compositions should show.

Fifth Grade: Big Elements—Interdisciplinary Connections

In the fifth-grade year, the students compose music for, and compile, an entire CD. It is truly interdisciplinary in that it is based on, and inspired by famous artworks as well as their own art, and they write their biographies and liner notes for the CDs. Mrs. Andrews, the language arts teacher, helps them write their biographies and liner notes that describe their music, and Mr. Toma, the art teacher, has been guiding the students to carefully select a portfolio of artworks to inspire their music, as well as to design their CD cover.

Today the students are broken into three groups: some of the students are in the art room finishing up the art for the CD cover; another group is working in the computer lab typing their liner notes; and the third group is in the music room, using the recording equipment to record some of their original compositions.

Keira has been intrigued by the stillness of Mark Rothko's paintings, and even more so by Morton Feldman's music compositions that were inspired by Rothko's artwork (on

Feldman's CD *Rothko's Chapel*). She composed a piece of music she titled "Calm," for five players on Alto Orff instruments. This was inspired by a particular painting by Rothko titled *Orange and Yellow*. Her music, like the painting, is seemingly static as the players move through a progression of very slow moving sustained chords. Mr. Grainger had just been teaching about "tension and release" in music class, and as he was watching her rehearse her classmates, he commented: "Oh Keira, you are showing such patience with this! The tension becomes almost unbearable with the slow chords. Do you want to do anything to release the tension?" Keira thought a bit as she recalled the lesson they completed during the week on ostinato as a tension builder. "No, I don't think so, Mr. Grainger. But I do think I need to add some dynamics to build up and then fade away at the end." She asked her players to mark their scores with some dynamic markings before they commenced with their final run-through before recording.

Fifth grade is also the year that students can elect to join the band or orchestra. Here students will apply their developing composition skills as they compose the songs they will perform on their first concert in December. The band and orchestra teacher, Ms. Carmody, enjoys the enthusiasm that the students bring toward improvising and composing songs when they join one of the ensembles. The first few weeks of band and orchestra are focused on learning the physical techniques of holding and manipulating the instruments as well as developing good tone quality. The students learn by ear, and as they add new notes to their repertoire, they compose simple songs, either individually or as an ensemble. Ms. Carmody will not introduce written repertoire or books until after the fundamental physical techniques and tone qualities are solid.

Imagine

Imagine a year of music moving in the direction of the "Music Utopia Elementary School," as described above: class begins with improvisation, continues with the concept(s) of the day, and then students compose or improvise around the concept to be learned. School concerts include a mixture of compositions composed by the students as well as the usual repertoire performed in elementary school. As students learn to improvise and compose, their understanding of and appreciation for already composed music will only deepen.

Imagine collaborating with the language arts teacher and the visual arts teacher on creating an original "musical story," complete with visual artwork, to be performed for parents in the spring. The approach to the curriculum is organic, with lessons stemming from questions and opportunities based on students' interest and natural evolution in composition. What happens when you bang two pieces of wood together compared to pieces of metal? Which sounds do you prefer, and why? Compose a song of ugly sounds. Compose a song of beautiful sounds. Compose a song of sounds that move from beautiful to ugly. It should have a steady beat as well as be in a triple feel. Work with a partner to create music that contrasts meters and sounds. What happens to the feeling of the music when the time changes? How might you notate it? Are there easier ways? What happens to the development of clean and clear tonal and rhythmic patterns?

Although the vignettes of music learning at MUES might seem extreme, they were inspired by real music teachers I have seen work this magic in their classrooms. I hope that they spark ideas for lessons that put creative musical thinking and doing at the center of learning in order to engage deeper musical thought from students. Composition, improvisation, and creative exploration activities lead to qualitatively deeper understandings than "re-creating" music. Although the norm is to teach students the "outside-in" version of music (that is, we give them the musical things they are supposed to learn), students who compose experience an "inside-out" view of music. In this organic and creative approach to curriculum, there is less focus on teaching the facts and bits of the (somewhat contrived) elements of melody, rhythm, texture, harmony, with careful sequencing of sol-la before ti-do (for instance), than there is on simply making music in a joyful manner, and teaching about the music after it is composed. It means starting from the whole that is made up and imagined by children, then dissecting and analyzing that organic whole into parts, and then moving out to the whole again.

The Spiral Approach

"A curriculum as it develops should revisit these basic ideas repeatedly, building upon them until the student has grasped the full formal apparatus that goes with them" (Bruner, 1960, p. 13). Jerome Bruner profoundly affected education and curriculum when he introduced the concept that children can learn any subject at any age as long as it is presented in terms that are relevant and meaningful to them. Whereas the previous chapters in this book provide a variety of possible composition and improvisation activities, Bruner's spiral curriculum model provides a potential structure from which to enact them. A spiral curriculum approach with music creativity included in the core, as diagrammed in figure 8.1, centers around music listening, performing, composing, and improvising. Mr. Grainger, the fictitious teacher at MUES, would use a spiral curriculum in which he touches on concepts each year and "grows" them by revisiting them at a deeper and more complex level as children develop. The means by which these are taught in the creative approach to music are through improvisation and composition. These creative activities form the core of the curriculum and help to form the other concepts we teach in music, such as the context of music, the musical elements, and music history.

Creativity at the Core of School Music

—In composition, to produce is first of all to take pleasure in the production of differences. (Attali, 1985, p. 142)

Children come to school with years of musical experience under their belts. However, sometimes we approach students as if they do not "know" music and it is our job, as teacher,

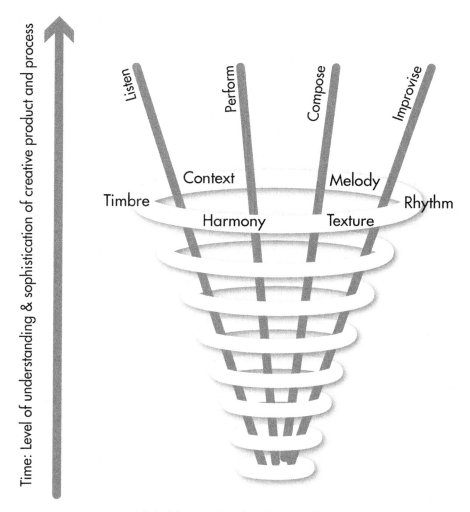

FIGURE 8.1 A Spiral Approach to Creative Teaching and Learning

to teach them music. We forget that their home environments are likely full of rich and complex musical sounds, and have been since they were born. We also forget they have the ability to make their own music, just as they can make up stories and paint pictures. Students come to school full of music: musical ideas, musical rhythms, musical facts, musical love, and musical experiences. And their knowledge of music might be richer now than ever before in history because of the ubiquitous digital music players and other sound sources that provide immediate and constant access to music.

Not only do students come to school with extensive musical backgrounds, but we also know from research that children *can* compose and enjoy doing so.[2] There does not seem to be a consistent "how-to" formula, and in fact many teachers have learned that a student-centered and emergent approach to the process of teaching composition is the most satisfying. Learning to allow students' unique voices and identities to emerge seems the most important skill a teacher can possess.

An important part of the equation is the teacher, who must have the disposition to teach in an evolving and organic manner. The ability to improvise in the moment, allowing student ideas to emerge and shape the learning experience, is important for successful composition teaching (Bolden, 2009; Gould, 2006; Ruthmann, 2008). "Just as there is no one right way to compose, there is no one right way to teach or evaluate compositions. Instead, both the teacher and the composer must approach composition as a problem-solving exercise" (Younker, 2003, p. 237). In order to implement a curriculum with creative musical activities at the core, a teacher must be flexible and skillful. He or she must have the ability to gently "manage" a class while at the same time provide space for musical chaos. It becomes an artful balance between freedom and control. And music teachers must be able to think imaginatively in order to teach from a curriculum in which the "repertoire" comes from the students.

The core of all music teaching should come from the creative essence of music. It begins by organizing the curriculum with the end goals in mind, but must follow a map through the unknown territories that composition and improvisation will bring.

Artistry

Finally, and perhaps most important, we must not forget the importance of artistry in making music. It is easy and fun to create an "anything goes" attitude in creative music making, with final compositions deemed successful simply because they are finished. Although wild experimentation and silly-sounding compositions are appropriate at times, we must keep a thread of our focus on developing aesthetic sensitivity and a sense of artistry in our students. Reimer (1989) presents a set of criteria for making quality judgments about a work of art: craftsmanship, sensitivity, imagination, and authenticity. Craftsmanship involves the ability to put materials of art together in a way that creates expressiveness in the product. Sensitivity becomes manifest through the depth of feeling that is inherent in the music. Imagination reveals a refreshing originality in the artwork. And authenticity relates to the "genuineness of the artist's interaction with his materials" (p. 138). If we keep these in mind as goals when teaching music composition, and share these criteria with our students, then we will develop students who are not only musically creative, but critical, artistic, and sensitive musical thinkers as well. Just as we strive for artistry in performance, we should also strive for developing artistry through music composition. Reaching artistry, just as achieving any goal of merit, takes work, persistence, patience, and much practice. Music composition requires this and more, at the same time it provides an outlet for children that will offer them rewards beyond the norm.

I hope that the activities and ideas outlined in this book help teachers to realize that composing and improvising in the classroom is not nearly as difficult as they might have been led to believe. Composing is simply organizing sound and silence in feelingful ways. Standard notation is not a prerequisite, and sounds do not have to fit neatly into a steady 4-beat pattern. Try out the activities presented in this book, and begin to trust the natural creative impulses of the students. Build a repertoire of composition and improvisation techniques and activities, and develop them further each year. Once we have opened up our ears to the vast possibilities of what music is and can be, then the options for composition and improvisation in the classroom are infinite. And the musical experiences for the students will be enriched beyond our imagination.

Notes

CHAPTER 1

1. Performing other's music as a separate act from composing or improvising is new in our Western culture. For historical overviews on this phenomenon, see Pressing (1988), Attali (1985), and Small (1998). Outside of the Western canon, it is not unusual at all for creation and music making to be a singular act.

2. The *students* I refer to throughout this book are those whom I have taught over the years and include children in K–12 settings as well as preservice and in-service teachers.

3. Chapter 3 provides specific listening and exploration activities to help stimulate this discussion toward a definition.

4. Composing *well* or in a creative manner is an altogether different, yet important issue that I will discuss later.

5. This motivation toward exploration and process over product by young children may explain why, in my own work and that of Stauffer (2002, 2003), I have found that younger children are more reluctant to revise their final musical composition than older and more experienced student composers. Webster (2003) provides ideas for encouraging revision processes with younger composers.

CHAPTER 2

1. An activity is intrinsically motivated when self-initiated or taken on for personal satisfaction; extrinsic motivation drives one to complete an activity because of a tangible reward given by another person.

2. Table 2.1 provides a very simplified and gross generalization of a very complicated topic. The personality of the teacher, the students, and the cultural and social context of the classroom all provide confounding variables to this complex area of motivation and creativity. This simplification, however, provides a place to start when thinking about the types of composition assignments and parameters teachers give. At the very least, if we continually find ourselves in the "same box," then we are doing a disservice to the types of learners who prefer, and might be motivated by, a different style. For a more recent review of the research on motivation and creativity see Ryan and Deci (2000).

3. Perhaps the best source dedicated to this issue is *Can I Play You My Song?* by Rena Upitis (1992). Upitis outlines the research on learners' natural development of notation understanding and writing. Upitis also offers practical ideas for collecting and understanding children's music notations, as well as advice for moving children naturally toward an understanding of standard notation through music composition. For teachers or researchers interested in this topic, the Upitis book is highly recommended.

4. Seymour Papert coined the terms "letteracy" and "letterate" to define the traditional ways one is able to read and write. He defines the terms *literacy* and *literate* to mean more holistic "ways of knowing" in a domain. "Becoming literate means thinking differently than one did previously, seeing the world differently, and this suggests that there are many different literacies" (Papert, 1993, p. 10).

5. Both notation and sequencing software allow a user to record, play back, and print music with or without the aid of a MIDI synthesizer. The main purpose of notation software is for printing music, whereas the main

purpose of sequencing software is for recording music. Now it is not uncommon for software programs to provide both features.

6. One could present a compelling argument here for the use of computer technology taking over the need to learn to write standard notation.

7. Amabile coined the phrase "consensual assessment" through her studies that used this technique for rating visual artwork (see Amabile, 1979, 1996; Hennessy & Amabile, 1988).

8. Alfie Kohn's (1993) book *Punished by Rewards: The Trouble with Gold Stars, Incentive Plans, A's, Praise, and Other Bribes* presents a comprehensive and fascinating review of research on this topic.

9. *Lessons from a Child* (1983) was Calkins's first and most influential book on the teaching of writing to children. Subsequent books, such as *The Art of Teaching Writing* (1994) and *One to One: The Art of Conferring with Young Writers* (Calkins, Harman, & White, 2005), provide invaluable insights into guiding the creative working process of children with ideas that work equally well with creative music writing.

CHAPTER 3

1. A recording that really forces thought on this question is music played by elephants on the audio CD *Thai Elephant Orchestra*.

2. Ideas for these journals are described in more detail in lesson 3F.

3. The Eberle (1996) book contains several visual imagination exercises that would adapt well to musical imagination.

CHAPTER 4

1. This particular facility was a group home for young men who were identified as "high-needs" and, for a variety of reasons ranging from absent parents to safety, were not able to live in their own homes.

2. For more information about my work with these particular students, see Hickey (2009).

3. The term "songs" was most often used to depict music with lyrics. However, depending on the circumstance and the student, "song" was also interchangeably used with "music" and "beats."

CHAPTER 5

1. In the literature on writing (or teaching to write) fiction, the beginning is often called a *lead*. For suggestions on writing good leads, see http://teacher.scholastic.com/lessonrepro/lessonplans/instructor/power.htm.

CHAPTER 6

1. When I use the term "good" here, I mean to describe a melody or music that follows all of the proper rules in the Western tonal tradition and seems to be appealing to audiences (it stands the test of time).

2. The term *beat* is pervasive in the culture of some of the urban students I teach. They will often use it in place of the term *music*. To them, composing music means writing beats.

CHAPTER 8

1. The article in the edited book was first published in the *New York Times*, April 23, 1933, education section, p. 7, from an address by Dewey on April 21, 1933, at the "Conference on the Educational Status of the Four- and Five-Year-Old Child," Teachers College, Columbia University. See Dewey (2008/1933).

2. See Hickey (2012) for a review of recent research on teaching music composition to children.

References

Allen, P. (2002). *Composing matters*. Oxford, UK: Heinemann Educational.

Amabile, T. M. (1979). Effects of external evaluation on artistic creativity. *Journal of Personality and Social Psychology, 37*(2), 221–233.

Amabile, T. M. (1996). *Creativity in context: Update to the social psychology of creativity*. Boulder, CO: Westview Press.

Arieti, S. (1976). *Creativity: The magic synthesis*. New York: Basic Books.

Astington, J. W., & Olson, D. R. (1995). The cognitive revolution in children's understanding of mind. *Human Development, 38,* 203–213.

Attali, J. (1985). *Noise: The political economy of music*. Minneapolis: University of Minnesota Press.

Bamberger, J. (1991). *The mind behind the musical ear: How children develop musical intelligence*. Cambridge, MA: Harvard University Press.

Bangs, R. L. (1992). An application of Amabile's model of creativity to music instruction: A comparison of motivational strategies. PhD diss., University of Miami, Coral Gables, Florida.

Barrett, J. R., McCoy, C. S., & Veblen, K. K. (1997). *Sound ways of knowing: Music in the interdisciplinary curriculum*. New York: Schirmer Books.

Barrett, M. (1996). Children's aesthetic decision-making: An analysis of children's musical discourse as composers. *International Journal of Music Education, 28,* 37–61.

Benson, W. (1967). *Creative projects in musicianship: A report of pilot projects sponsored by the Contemporary Music Project at Ithaca College and Interlochen Arts Academy. CMP4*. Washington, DC: MENC.

Berger, A. A., & Cooper, S. (2003). Musial play: A case study of preshool children and parents. *Journal of Research in Music Education, 51*(2), 151–165.

Bernstein, L. (1966). *The infinite variety of music*. New York: Simon and Schuster.

Blair, D. V. (2007). Musical maps as narrative inquiry. *International Journal of Education & the Arts, 8*(15). Retrieved January 16, 2010, from http://www.ijea.org/v8n15/.

Bolden, B. (2009). Teaching composing in secondary school: A case study analysis. *British Journal of Music Education, 26*(2), 137–152.

Borland, J. H. (1988). Cognitive controls, cognitive styles, and divergent production in gifted preadolescents. *Journal for the Education of the Gifted, 11,* 57–82.

Bramhall, D. (1989). *Composing in the classroom. Opus 1 & 2*. London: Boosey & Hawkes.

Brinkman, D. J. (1999). Problem finding, creativity style and musical compositions of high school students. *Journal of Creative Behavior, 33*(1), 62–68.

Brown, E. (2008). On December 1952. *American Music, 26*(1), p. 1–12.

Bruner, J. (1960). *The process of education*. Cambridge, MA: Harvard University Press.

Burnard, P. (2000). How children ascribe meaning to improvisation and composition: Rethinking pedagogy in music education. *Music Education Research, 2*(1), 7–23.

Burnard, P., & Younker, B. A. (2004). Problem-solving and creativity: Insights from students' individual composing pathways. *International Journal of Music Education, 22,* 59–75.

Burrows, M. (2007). *Outside the lines: A new approach to composing in the classroom.* Dayton, OH: Heritage Music Press.

Burton, L. (1990). Comprehensive musicianship: The Hawaii music curriculum project. *The Quarterly, 1*(3), 67–76.

Cage, J. (1961). *Silence: Lectures and writings by John Cage.* Middletown, CT: Wesleyan University Press.

Calkins, L. M. (1983). *Lessons from a child: On the teaching and learning of writing.* Portsmouth, NH: Heinemann.

Calkins, L. M. (1994). *The art of teaching writing* (2nd ed.). Portsmouth, NH: Heinemann.

Calkins, L. M., Hartman, A., & White, Z. R. (2005). *One to one: The art of conferring with young writers.* Portsmouth, NH: Heinemann.

Camphouse, M. (Ed.). (2002). *Composers on composing for band.* Chicago, IL: GIA.

Claire, L. (1993/1994). The social psychology of creativity: The importance of peer social processes for students' academic and artistic creative activity in classroom contexts. *Bulletin of the Council for Research in Music Education, 119,* 21–28.

Contemporary Music Project. (1965). *Comprehensive musicianship: A report of the seminar sponsored by the Contemporary Music Project at Northwestern University, April, 1965. CMP 2.* Washington, DC: MENC.

Contemporary Music Project. (1966). *Experiments in musical creativity: A report of pilot projects sponsored by the Contemporary Music Project in Baltimore, San Diego, and Farmingdale. CMP 3.* Washington, DC: MENC.

Copland, A. (1985/1939). *What to listen for in music.* New York: Mentor.

Cutietta, R. A. (1993). The musical elements, who said they're right? *Music Educators Journal, 79*(9), 48–53.

Davidson, L., & Scripp, L. (1988). Young children's musical representations: Windows on music. In J. Sloboda (Ed.), *Generative processes in music: The psychology of performance, improvisation and composition* (pp. 195–230). Oxford, England: Clarendon.

Davies, C. D. (1986). Say it till a song comes (reflections on songs invented by children 3–13). *British Journal of Research in Music Education, 3*(3), 279–293.

Davies, C. D. (1992). Listen to my song: a study of songs invented by children aged 5 to 7 years. *British Journal of Music Education, 9,* 19–48.

Davies, C. D. (1994). The listening teacher: An approach to the collection and study of invented songs of children aged 5 to 7. In H. Lees (Ed.), *Musical connections: Tradition and change. Proceedings of the 21st world conference of the International Society of Music Education* (pp. 120–128). Tampa, FL: ISME.

Davis, G. A. (2004). *Creativity is forever* (5th ed.). Dubuque, IA: Kendall/Hunt.

Deci, E. L., Koestner, R., & Ryan, R. M. (2001). Extrinsic rewards and intrinsic motivation in education: Reconsidered once again. *Review of Educational Research, 71*(1), 1–29.

DeLorenzo, L. C. (1989). A field study of sixth-grade students' creative music problem-solving processes. *Journal of Research in Music Education, 37*(3), 188–200.

Dewey, J. (2008/1933). Dewey outlines utopian schools. In J. A. Boydston (ed.), *The later works of John Dewey, Volume 9, 1925–1953: 1933–1934, essays, reviews, miscellany, and a common faith* (pp. 136–140). Carbondale: Southern Illinois University Press.

Dillon, J. T. (1982). Problem finding and solving. *Journal of Creative Behavior, 16*(2), 97–111.

Dunn, R. E. (1997). Creative thinking and music listening. *Research Studies in Music Education, 8,* 1–16.

Eberle, B. (1996). *SCAMPER: Games for imagination development.* Waco, TX: Prufrock Press.

Eisenberger, R., & Cameron, J. (1998). Reward, intrinsic interest, and creativity: New findings. *American Psychologist, 53*(6), 676–679.

Evans, G. (2003). *Music inspired by art: A guide to recordings.* Lanham, MD: Scarecrow Press.

Feist, G. J. (1999). The influence of personality on artistic and scientific creativity. In R. J. Sternberg (Ed.), *Handbook of creativity* (pp. 273–296). Cambridge: Cambridge University Press.

Flohr, J. W. (1985). Young children's improvisations: Emerging creative thought. *Creative Child and Adult Quarterly, 10*(2), 79–85.

Flohr, J. W. (2005). *The musical lives of young children.* Upper Saddle River, NJ: Prentice Hall.

Folger, R., Rosenfield, D., & Hays, R. P. (1976). Equity and intrinsic motivation: The role of choice. *Journal of Personality and Social Psychology, 36*(5), 557–564.

Gardner, H. (1993). *Creating minds: An anatomy of creativity seen through the lives of Freud, Einstein, Picasso, Stravinsky, Eliot, Graham, and Gandhi.* New York: Basic Books.

Getzels, J. W., & Csikszentmihalyi, M. (1976). *The creative vision: A longitudinal study of problem finding in art.* New York: Wiley.

Gould, E. (2006). Dancing composition: Pedagogy and philosophy as experience. *International Journal of Music Education, 24*(3), 197–207.

Hargreaves, D. J. (1984). The effects of repetition on like for music. *Journal of Research in Music Education, 32*(1), 35–47.

Harvey, J. (1999). *Music and inspiration.* New York: Faber and Faber.

Hebert, E. A. (2001). *The power of portfolios: What children can teach us about learning and assessment.* San Francisco, CA: Jossey-Bass.

Hennessey, B. A. (2000). Rewards and creativity. In C. Sansone & J. M. Harackiewicz (Eds.), *Intrinsic and extrinsic motivation: The search for optimal motivation and performance* (pp. 55–78). San Diego: Academic Press.

Hennessey, B. A., & Amabile, T. M. (1988). The conditions of creativity. In R. J. Sternberg (Ed.), *The nature of creativity* (pp. 11–38). New York: Cambridge University Press.

Hickey, M. (1995). *Qualitative and Quantitative Relationships Between Children's Creative Musical Thinking Processes and Products.* PhD diss., Northwestern University, Evanston, IL.

Hickey, M. (2001). An application of Amabile's consensual assessment technique for rating the creativity of children's musical compositions. *Journal of Research in Music Education, 49*(3), 234–244.

Hickey, M. (Ed.). (2003). *Why and how to teach music composition: A new horizon for music education.* Reston, VA: MENC.

Hickey, M. (2009). At-risk teens: Making sense of life through music composition. In J. L. Kerchner & C. Abril (Eds.), *Musical experience in our lives: Things we learn and meanings we make* (pp. 199–216). Lanham, MD: Rowman & Littlefield.

Hickey, M. (2012). What pre-service teachers can learn from composition research. In M. Kaschub & J. Smith (Eds.), *Composing our future: Preparing music educators to teach composition.* New York: Oxford University Press.

Hickey, M., & Reese, S. (2001). The development of a rating scale for judging constructive feedback for student compositions. *Journal of Technology in Music Learning, 1*(1), 10–19.

Hillocks, G. (1975). *Observing and writing.* Urbana, IL: National Council of Teachers of English. (ERIC Document Reproduction Service No. ED102574).

Howard, J. (1990). *Learning to compose.* Cambridge: Cambridge University Press.

Jarrett, S., & Day, H. (2008). *Music composition for dummies.* Hoboken, NJ: Wiley.

Johns, G. A., Morse, L. W., & Morse, D. T. (2001). An analysis of early vs. later responses on a divergent production task across three time press conditions. *Journal of Creative Behavior, 35*(1), 65–72.

Kaschub, M. (1997). A comparison of two composer-guided large group composition projects. *Research Studies in Music Education, 8,* 15–28.

Kaschub, M., & Smith, J. (2009). *Minds on music: Composition for creative and critical thinking.* Reston, VA: Rowman & Littlefield Education.

Keene, J. A. (1982). *A history of music education in the United States.* Hanover, NH: University Press of New England.

Kerchner, J. L. (2000). Children's verbal, visual, and kinesthetic responses: Insight into their music listening experience. *Bulletin of the Council for Research in Music Education, 146,* 31–50.

Kohn, A. (1993). *Punished by rewards: The trouble with gold stars, incentive plans, A's, praise, and other bribes.* Boston, MA: Houghton Mifflin.

Lely, J., & Saunders, J. (2012). *Word events: perspectives on verbal notation.* London, England: Continuum.

Levi, R. (1991). Investigating the creativity process: The role of regular music composition experiences for the elementary child. *Journal of Creative Behavior, 25*(2), 123–136.

Littleton, D. (1991). *Influence of play settings on preschool children's music and play behaviors.* Ph.D. diss., University of Texas at Austin.

Lowenfeld, V., & Brittain, W. L. (1987). *Creative and mental growth* (8th ed.). Englewood Cliffs, NJ: Prentice-Hall.

MacDonald, R. & Miell, D. (2000). Creativity and music education: The impact of social variables. *International Journal of Music Education, 36,* 58–68.

Mark, M. L. (1996). *Contemporary music education* (3rd ed.). New York: Schirmer Books.

Marsh, K. (1995). Children's singing games: composition in the playground? *Research Studies in Music Composition, 4,* 2–11.

Marsh, K., & Young, S. (2006). Musical play. In G. E. McPherson (Ed.), *The child as musician. A handbook of musical development* (pp. 298–310). New York: Oxford University Press.

May, R. (1994). *The courage to create.* New York: Norton & Company.

Mayer, R. E. (1999). Fifty years of creativity research. In R. J. Sternberg (Ed.), *Handbook of creativity* (pp. 449–460). Cambridge: Cambridge University Press.

McDonald, D. T., & Simons, G. M. (1989). *Musical growth and development: Birth through six.* New York: Schirmer Books.

Meyer, L. (1961). *Emotion and meaning in music.* Chicago: University of Chicago Press.

Miller, R. F. (1992). Affective response. In R. Colwell (Ed.), *Handbook of research on music teaching and learning* (pp. 414–424). New York: Schirmer Books.

Moorhead, G., & Pond, D. (1978). *Music for young children.* Santa Barbara: Pillsbury Foundation for the Advancement of Music Education (reprinted from the 1941–1951 editions).

Morse, D. T., Morse, L. W., & Johns, G. A. (2001). Do time press, stimulus, and creative prompt influence the divergent production of undergraduate students? Yes, Yes, and No, Not very much. *Journal of Creative Behavior, 35*(2), 102–114.

Mumford, M. D., Feldman, J. M., Hein, M. B., & Nagao, D. J. (2001). Tradeoffs between ideas and structure: Individual versus group performance in creative problem solving. *Journal of Creative Behavior, 35*(1), 1–23.

Music Educators National Conference. (1994). *The school music program: A new vision. The K–12 National Standards, PreK Standards, and what they mean to music educators.* Reston, VA: MENC.

Music Educators National Conference. (1996). *Performance standards for music. Grades PreK–12.* Reston, VA: MENC.

Music Educators National Conference. (2001). *Benchmark Student Performances in Music: Composing and Arranging.* Reston, VA: MENC.

Nettl, B. (1974). Thoughts on improvisation: A comparative approach. *The Musical Quarterly, 60*(1), 1–19.

Oliveros, P. (1974). *Sonic meditations.* Troy, NY: Deep Listening Institute.

Oliveros, P. (2005). *Deep listening: A composer's sound practice.* Lincoln, NE: iUniverse.

Papert, S. (1993). *The children's machine. Rethinking school in the age of the computer.* New York: Basic Books.

Paulson, J. (1975). *Epinicion* (For concert band; Conservatory Editions; Grade 5; Score and set of parts). San Diego, CA: Neil A. Kjos Music.

Paynter, J. (1992). *Sound and structure.* Cambridge: Cambridge University Press.

Paynter, J., & Aston, P. (1970). *Sound and silence: Classroom projects in creative music.* Cambridge: Cambridge University Press.

Peterik, J, Austin, D., & Bickford, M. E. (2002). *Songwriting for dummies.* New York: Wiley Press.

Piirto, J. (1998). *Understanding those who create* (2nd ed.). Scottsdale, AZ: Great Potential Press.

Pressing, J. (1988). Improvisation: Methods and models. In J. Sloboda (Ed.), *Generative processes in music: The psychology of performance, improvisation and composition* (pp. 129–178). Oxford, England: Clarendon.

Reese, S. (2003). Responding to student compositions. In M. Hickey (Ed.), *Music composition in the schools: A new horizon for music education* (pp. 211–232). Reston, VA: MENC.

Reimer, B. (1989). *A philosophy of music education* (2nd ed.). Englewood Cliffs, NJ: Prentice Hall.

Runco, M. A. (Ed.). (1994). *Problem finding, problem solving, and creativity.* Norwood, NJ: Ablex.

Runco, M. A. (1996). Personal creativity: Definition and developmental issues. In M. A. Runco (Ed.), *Creativity from childhood through adulthood: The developmental issues* (pp. 3–30). San Francisco: Jossey-Bass.

Runco, M. A., & Chand, I. (1995). Cognition and creativity. *Educational Psychology Review, 7*(3), 243–267.

Russ, S. W. (1996). Development of creative processes in children. In M. A. Runco (Ed.), *Creativity from childhood through adulthood: The developmental issues* (pp. 31–42). San Francisco: Jossey-Bass.

Ruthmann, S. A. (2008). Whose agency matters? Negotiating pedagogical and creative intent during composing experiences. *Research Studies in Music Education, 30*(1), 43–58.

Ryan, R. M., & Deci, E. L. (2000). Intrinsic and extrinsic motivations: Classic definitions and new directions. *Contemporary Educational Psychology, 25*(1), 54–67.

Sapp, D. P. (1997). Problem parameters and problem finding in art education. *Journal of Creative Behavior, 31*(4), 282–298.

Sauer, T. (2009). *Notations 21.* New York: Mark Batty.

Sawyer, R. K. (2006). Educating for innovation. *Thinking Skills and Creativity, 1*, 41–48.

Schafer, R. M. (1986). *The thinking ear.* Ontario, Canada: Arcana Editions.

Schafer, R. M. (1992). *A sound education.* Ontario, Canada: Arcana Editions.

Schoenberg, A. (1984). *Style and idea: Selected writings of Arnold Schoenberg.* Edited by L. Stein. Berkeley: University of California Press.

Schubert, W. H. (2009). *Love, justice, and education: John Dewey and the Utopians.* Charlotte, NC: Information Age.

Sessions, R. (1950). *The musical experience of composer, performer, listener.* Princeton, NJ: Princeton University Press.

Simonton, D. K. (1987). Musical aesthetic and creativity in Beethoven: A computer analysis of 105 compositions. *Empirical Studies of the Arts, 5,* 87–104.

Simonton, D. K. (1991). Emergence and realization of genius: The lives and woks of 120 classical composers. *Journal of Personality and Social Psychology, 61,* 829–840.

Simonton, D. K. (1999). Creativity from a historiometric perspective. In R. J. Sternberg (Ed.), *Handbook of creativity* (pp. 116–33). Cambridge: Cambridge University Press.

Small, C. (1998). *Musicking. The meaning of performing and listening.* Middletown, CT: Wesleyan University Press.

Smithrim, K. L. (1997). Free musical play in early childhood. *Canadian Music Educator, 38*(4), 17–22.

Soep, E. (1996). An art in itself: Youth development through critique. *Noir Designs, 12,* 42–46.

Stauffer, S. (2002). Connections between the musical and life experiences of young composers and their compositions. *Journal of Research in Music Education, 50*(4), 301–322.

Stauffer, S. (2003). Identity and voice in young composers. In, M. Hickey (Ed.), *Music composition in the schools: A new horizon for music education* (pp. 91–112). Reston, VA: MENC.

Sternberg, R. J., & Lubart, T. I. (1991). An investment theory of creativity and its development. *Human Development, 34*(1), 1–32.

Stevens, J. (2007). *Search and reflect: A music workshop handbook.* Middlesex, UK: Rock School Limited.

Thomas, R. B. (1970). *Manhattanville music curriculum program: Final report.* Washington, DC: U.S. Office of Education, Bureau of Research. ERIC document ED 045 865.

Tsisserev, A. (1997). *An ethnography of secondary school student composition in music—a study of personal involvement within the compositional process.* PhD diss., University of British Columbia.

Upitis, R. (1990). *This too is music!* Portsmouth, NH: Heinemann.

Upitis, R. (1992). *Can I play you my song? The compositions and invented notations of children.* Portsmouth, NH: Heinemann.

Vella, R. (2003). *Sounds in space, sounds in time: Projects in listening, improvising and composing.* London: Boosey & Hawkes.

Vergo, P. (2010). *The music of painting.* London: Phaidon Press.

Wakefield, J. F. (1985). Towards creativity: Problem finding in a divergent-thinking exercise. *Children Study Journal, 15,* 265–270.

Wakefield, J. F. (1991). The outlook for creativity tests. *Journal of Creative Behavior, 25*(3), 184–193.

Wakefield, J. F. (1994). Problem finding and empathy in art. In M. A. Runco (Ed.), *Problem finding, problem solving, and creativity* (pp. 99–115). Norwood, NJ: Ablex.

Wallas, G. (1926). *The art of thought.* New York: Harcourt, Brace and World.

Webster, P. (1990). Creativity as creative thinking. *Music Educators Journal, 76*(9), 22–28.

Webster, P. (2003). Asking music students to reflect on their creative work: Encouraging the revision process. *Music Education Research, 5*(3), 243–248.

Wiggins, J. H. (1994). Children's strategies for solving compositional problems with peers. *Journal of Research in Music Education, 42*(3), 232–252.

Wiggins, J. H. (2000). The nature of shared musical understanding and its role in empowering independent musical thinking. *Bulletin of the Council for Research in Music Education, 143,* 65–90.

Wiggins, J. H. (2003). A frame for understanding children's compositional processes. In M. Hickey (Ed.), *Music composition in the schools: A new horizon for music education* (pp. 141–166). Reston, VA: MENC.

Younker, B. A. (2000). Thought processes and strategies of students engaged in music composition. *Research Studies in Music Education, 14*(1), 24–39.

Younker, B. A. (2003). The nature of feedback in a community of composing. In M. Hickey (Ed.), *Why and how to teach music composition: A new horizon for music education* (pp. 233–242). Reston, VA: Rowman & Littlefield Education.

Younker, B. A. (2006). Reflective practice through the lens of a fifth grade composition-based music class. In P. Burnard & S. Hennessy (Eds.), *Reflective practices in arts education* (pp. 159–168). Dordrecht, Netherlands: Springer.

Index

CPSIA information can be obtained at www.ICGtesting.com
Printed in the USA
BVOW09s0315070716

454713BV00005B/14/P